THE MASTER ARCHITECT SERIES

TERRY FARRELL

Selected and Current Works

TERRY FARRELL

Selected and Current Works

First published in Australia in 1994 by
The Images Publishing Group Pty Ltd
ACN 059 734 431
6 Bastow Place, Mulgrave, Victoria, 3170
Telephone (61 3) 561 5544 Facsimile (61 3) 561 4860

National Library of Australia Cataloguing-in-Publication Data

    Farrell, Terry, 1938–.
       Terry Farrell: selected and current works.

       Bibliography.
       Includes index.
       ISBN 1 875498 16 8.
       Master Architect Series ISSN 1320 7253

       1. Farrell, Terry, 1938–. 2. Architecture, Modern—20th
       century—Great Britain. 3. Architecture, British. 4. Architects—
       Great Britain. I. Title. (Series: Master architect series).

720.92

Edited by Stephen Dobney
Designed by The Graphic Image Studio Pty Ltd,
Mulgrave, Australia
Printed by Southbank Book,
Fishermans Bend, Australia

Contents

Introduction

An Interview with Terry Farrell
by Clare Melhuish

You trained at Durham University and in the USA, and subsequently worked in the USA for a short period. What influence has your American experience/perspective brought to bear on your work, and do you believe it sets your work apart from that of other architects in this country?

I was in America at a time when cultural events in America were of great interest not only to the British but also throughout the world. It was a very strong time, when modern art, particularly the pop art movement, produced an original American culture, and when many writers and thinkers about the city, such as Louis Mumford, Jane Jacobs, or, in the field of ecology, Rachael Carson, were questioning the changes in our world produced by technology and urban growth. It was also a time of questioning in architecture at a more fundamental level than the Europeans had recently done. Buckminster Fuller, Louis Kahn and Bob Venturi were the three major contemporary figures that I was most interested in. These were all reasons for me to go to America, but I don't think that I brought back an American approach to architecture any more than did, say, Norman Foster and Richard Rogers, who were both students in America at the same time as I was, or Jim Stirling, Colin Rowe, and Alan Colquhoun, who were all visiting and teaching there. We each brought back our own different interpretations, and I think that what I brought back was an interest in a broader appreciation and understanding of art and architecture than the deliberate cultivation in Britain of art as an elitist concern. I also felt that there was a much more soundly based interest in technology in America, although while Bucky Fuller, Louis Kahn, or Mies in his later years looked at American technology and its potential, there was not the same little boy's love affair with technology that I would say identified the British attitude to it, and has gradually become more and more noticeable in British architecture. But the most profound influence on me, I think, was my learning experience on the extremely good urban design programme at the University of Pennsylvania, in an architecture and planning department run by people such as Louis Kahn. At the same time, Ed Bacons' work for the City of Philadelphia itself was a learning tool and experience, typical of the interchange between practice and education which takes place so readily in America. It was an enormously rich field of learning experience.

In conclusion I think that my feelings about America and my interpretation of America actually began before I ever went there. I think being at Durham University meant that I wasn't as influenced as people from London were by European traditions, particularly Le Corbusier, or the social engineering aspect of architecture that was so popular at London schools such as the Architectural Association. Durham was much more interested than southern schools at that time in Scandinavian architecture—the almost revisionist Modernism of Alto and Asplund—but also in American Modernism, such as the work of the west coast architects during the forties and fifties, plus Louis Kahn, of course, and others in the sixties. In addition I had an interest in a classless society which I think grew from my roots in the north of England, while the south still has a very strong class problem. This is visible in its elitist approach to architecture, embodied in the roles of the Arts Council, RIBA and Royal Fine Arts Commission. Going from Durham to America was a logical thing to do.

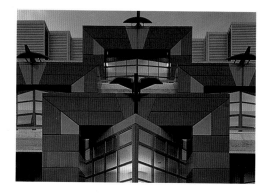

Your formative years were the 1960s, a time of great upheaval both in architectural and urban thinking and in society at large. Who, both in and outside architecture, were the most inspirational figures for you and your work; and what vision for the future of architecture did you have at that time?

Louis Kahn was an extraordinarily fine teacher, by far the greatest architectural educationalist I have ever come across. The experience of being with serious people in Philadelphia, such as Robert Venturi and Denise Scott Brown, and meeting Bucky Fuller several times was very inspiring. What I liked about Bucky was not only his interest in high-tech, but also his radicalism, his pioneering, one-man-band kind of radicalism. It was quite different to the European cult of radicalism, in which, in order to change things, you had to form a group like Archigram, the Mars Group or the Fabians. In America you get highly individual, not actually eccentric people, who really ploughed their own furrow. But my greatest interest in the fifties at architecture school and ever since has always been Frank Lloyd Wright, whom I consider the major architect of the last 100 years. He was outside all the major schools or extremes, yet he was greatly influenced by all that was going on in the world around him: he just re-interpreted it in a personal way. I also like the work of Saarinen and I was fascinated by the work of the students of Frank Lloyd Wright, such as Bruce Goff, Herb Green and many of those mid-west organic architects.

I came back and worked for a brief time for Colin Buchanan, and found his kind of very common-sense, simple approach to town planning fascinating. I particularly liked the excellence, and the quite beautiful presentation of books such as *Traffic in Towns* and other reports which he was involved in at the time. This use of the visual aid as a means of explanation in town planning and urban design has always been a great lesson to me. Other interesting characters were Archigram, Stirling and Gowan, and Cedric Price, and it was a very exciting time, but it was less that there were real individuals who were changing things, than a great mood of change, more like an atmosphere or an environment, that we were all part of. There is no doubt that both at school and in practice, my greatest interest was in formulating ideas about change and being outside the mainstream.

I enjoyed the early work at Farrell Grimshaw because it challenged the thinking of the day. In Britain in the fifties and sixties there was such a reliance upon heavyweight precast concrete brutalism, pretending to be very pro-social and changing society for the good. I thought it was basically anti-social, particularly the concrete housing estates and schools, the so-called rationalisation of the architecture of the welfare state, and I find it quite a disgusting period. What I enjoyed was proposing a different approach. When I got disenchanted, as I gradually did with the work of the high-tech school during the seventies, it was because it was becoming accepted as mainstream, but in the process becoming a businessman's architecture on the one hand, with buildings such as Willis Faber Dumas, and the industrial sheds of Farrell Grimshaw, and a cult architecture of taste on the other. It changed from being a servicing tool and a way of thinking to a much lesser thing. I particularly liked Ehrenkrantz's work at the time, which was almost anti-architecture, in comparison to the Pompidou Centre, which was an iconic thing, much more a

statement of style. High-tech became very much something for
the building owner to covet, with scant regard for function.
I regard Lloyds and Pompidou as sublimely impractical buildings
and the Hong Kong Shanghai Bank as an astonishingly
extravagant statement for an office building. I am as much
influenced by things I react against as I am by things that I am
attracted by, and in this respect I like to see myself as much more
a follower of Frank Lloyd Wright than a child of the sixties in the
high-tech groupie sense.

**You set up your partnership with Nicholas Grimshaw in 1965, and
it lasted for 15 years. Both you and he are now recognised as two
of the most prominent figures in current British architecture, but
during the eighties your work seemed to diverge in entirely
different directions. What were the common interests which
united you both during the sixties and seventies, and what were
the differences which eventually drew you apart?**

I think there are many misunderstandings about the work I was
doing during the sixties and seventies in the Farrell Grimshaw
Partnership. I was fascinated by the power of mass production on
the one hand, and on the other its potential for personalisation
and greater individual freedom, and how to make this
contradiction work. I wasn't in love with the mass-produced object
as many high-tech architects have become. I believed mass
production could provide the means for achieving great
adaptability to context and a very personalised response to the
user. It was these ideas which lay behind the projects for the
student hostel, Park Road flats, and the timber-framed housing
during the sixties and early to mid-seventies. It was really the
extent to which the partnership diverged between these two
interests, of architecture as product design on the one hand,
and my approach on the other, that began the split. So the
development of my own work has been quite consistent and
natural over the years. I believe that many who appear to be
working exclusively in one particular idiom do so because their
palette has not changed, when actually they have radically
changed their principles. By contrast, I have changed the palette,
the materials, and the kind of programmes, moving from housing
to large urban projects and master planning, but my principles
have remained the same, based on a belief in the potential of
technology to enrich the context and use of buildings.

**During the eighties, after the realisation of TVam, your name
became virtually synonymous with Post-Modernism in its British
form. Post-Modernism itself has now been pronounced by some
critics as "finished", implying that it was little more than a
transient fashion. What, for you, were or are the virtues of Post-
Modernism, and do you feel British criticism of the movement
was unjustified?**

Post-Modernism is interpreted totally differently from place to
place and from critic to critic, and the nature of these categories
and labels is not of particular interest. What is of interest is what
the work represents. My work has never been close to American
Post-Modernism, but rather to that of some European
Post-Modernists, such as Jim Stirling, Hollein, or Rossi. There is a
lot of confusion in Britain because of the strong anti-Americanism
of the cultural establishment, which is very deep-rooted, going
back before the war, and often accounted for, I think, by the fact

that Britain has always associated socialism with Modernism, and American capitalism as something of an enemy. Associated with that is the issue of working in the private versus the public sector. This gives a particular bias to readings of architecture in Britain which I find extremely tiresome. Basically I have always said that Post-Modernism is a way of seeing things, and recognising that the era of Modernism is over. It's "After-Modernism", not Post-Modernism, as a style that interested me. My work during the eighties represents a range of hybrid solutions, some of which are really quite high-tech. In some ways I was a pioneer during the eighties of many new materials and methods of construction and still am. Many a European and American critic has said that they can't understand why British critics have labelled me as a Post-Modernist because they see many parallels between my work and the typical British interest in construction.

The importance of the Post-Modernist era was to change the rules, to question the rut that Modernism had got into, and the idea that Modernists had that contemporary architecture could only be good if it was socially based or concerned with construction as product. In both cases these were only limited truths and I think that the eighties changed all that, in particular the understanding of the city and of urbanism, which Modernism had no grasp of at all. It did not have the scope to associate itself with Urbanism, because Urbanism involves context, and context involves the past and history, and it was the continuity of the past which was the very tenet Modernism set itself against in the 1920s.

So now, as Michael Graves said recently, we are all Post-Modernists: the spirit of Post-Modernism has influenced all architects and their work and in that sense it conquered all. I believe very strongly that the work of architects now has been enriched by the questioning that went on in the late seventies and eighties. I never really liked Post-Modernist style itself, but then I don't like any cult of a style; it is an individual's interpretation of what's going on around him which is much more interesting. It is this which makes Jim Stirling one of the most interesting so-called Post-Modernists, while Mario Botta, Hans Hollein and others also produced very exciting work which wasn't stylistically based. I think the identification of an American-style cult was just a way of labelling Americans; in fact it was a commercial phenomenon. It generated a lot of second-rate work in London, but then there is always second-rate work, whether it is Modernist or Post-Modernist or anything else.

Your interest in decoration, anthropomorphism, and the visual statement during this period clearly relates to your interest in the Arts and Crafts movement and Art Nouveau, which you state were inspired by the way things were made. How is this connection between visual appearance and technology developed in your own work?

My main aim is to try and design from the inside out as well as the outside in. My work is fundamentally based upon construction, use and function, as well as the influence of the context of the people and the place. At Charing Cross, Vauxhall Cross, or any of the other buildings there is a strong integration of the internal programme and the outer context. An architect's task is to develop form which follows function but also form following context. It is not a question of choosing between the two,

but of doing both, which requires more skill and creativity. It produces a more hybrid language and a cross-cultural type of building, but to try to produce an architecture which follows only one rule, whether constructional or functional, is simply escapist. It is partly a preoccupation with style, but it is also a way of over-simplifying a problem: making it so easy that a very major part of the equation is actually eliminated.

You have been closely involved with the rise of interest in conservation, the re-use of buildings and the exploration of low-tech. What is it about your work, in contrast to that of most other architects doing new architecture in a contemporary idiom, that has appealed to the conservation lobby in Britain, and led to your being appointed master planner for the new Paternoster Square scheme at St Paul's Cathedral, in which Prince Charles has taken some interest?

I am fascinated by an architecture that can raise a response of support, applause and love; by buildings that can bridge the gap between the elite and the populist causes. This is what Frank Lloyd Wright, Rennie Mackintosh, Boromini, Michelangelo, Soane, Wren and all the really great and enduring architects achieved. But in this century, perhaps because so many more people have been educated in the arts, many people have felt a need to set themselves apart and give themselves a sense of superiority by deliberately preferring an art that cannot be understood by others. It is this which started the search for an art of a deliberately limited appeal. I am not interested in that, but in trying to find an architecture which can be supported as much by the serious critic as the person in the street; because architecture is a public art, used by all kinds of people from the janitor on the door right up to the chairman in the boardroom, and there are so many more buildings that are publicly accessible—schools, libraries, art galleries and so on. To address populist issues as well as high culture is a major challenge of the day.

I must add here that the successive RIBA Presidents and the RIBA Director General spoke publicly against the Paternoster Square design, but it has now received, in the USA, the 1994 AIA Award for Urban Design—in my view a striking reflection of the parochial view of British taste.

You have spoken of the need for architecture to have symbolic content. Does this represent a search for the spiritual in an ever more material culture? And what, then, are the implications of cultural context for architecture? You are currently working in the Far East; do you think it is possible for a Western architect to create work rich in symbolic content for Eastern culture, with its very different cultural traditions and value systems?

I think that architecture always does have a symbolic content. What is not sufficiently recognised is that architecture always has a powerful symbolism. This is so often denied by architects, particularly by the Modernist establishment. They seem to have a kind of moral puritanism which sets out to deny the senses, as if by denying sensual experience in form, colour and shape, and exaggerating the importance of utilitarian function or a very limited view of user need, one frees oneself from any possible sensual or symbolic interpretation of one's work. There is much creativity in Britain which comes from the non-establishment and tolerant nature of the people here.

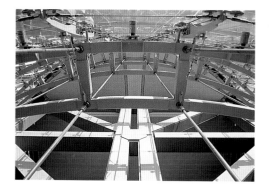

If one recognises that, in Freudian terms, there is always a reason, a motive, behind one's actions, then the symbolic content of architecture should be capable of interpretation in many different ways, some subconscious. Architecture should not be of a limited symbolic value, saying simply "I am powerful", or "I am clever", but a rich and varied thing, reflecting the range of culture and diverse needs of the democratic world that we live in. I have always been fascinated in the deep-rooted symbolic content of architecture, and in this Louis Kahn was a particularly strong influence. I think his fundamental Jewish background gave him a very deeply religious approach to architecture, in the broadest rather than a literal sense.

The basic elements of architecture—doorways, roofs, walls—are eternal and universal, each having a common cultural statement to make. But each gets adjusted and reinterpreted from region to region. For example, as one travels through the Far East, one meets with a different approach to the idea of permanence, so that the conservation movement in the West means something very different in the East. There it is not the built form itself which is handed down through generations, but the symbolic form: the dragon, the urn, the tea ceremony. The Shinto temples are demolished every 20 years to signify that religion is alive even if the temples are taken down and rebuilt. This very overt emphasis on the symbolic is a welcome thing. It doesn't necessarily mean that the symbols themselves are fundamentally different from those of Western culture, but there is a difference of emphasis. It gives one a completely new understanding of things that one has always taken for granted, and a great awareness of the commonality amongst mankind, despite the great differences. The further one travels, the greater perspective one gains on these almost primeval fundamental forces that are the essence of architecture.

In the end one is dealing with gravity, enclosure, climate and social tradition wherever one is, and it is very exciting to look at a train station in Hong Kong or a train station in Lisbon and see what is common and yet at the same time different. There are extraordinary disparities in context but it is the interchange, the interaction, between the general and the particular which is so interesting and exciting in architecture. One of the real issues of our time is the gradual erosion of cultural differences on a global scale, certainly as they are interpreted by mass production and mass culture. But I don't agree that the value systems of the East are fundamentally different from those of the West. Eastern cultures seem to have adapted to Western industrialisation and capitalism in many ways more rapidly and successfully than, say, the working classes of European countries, who were alienated by the 19th century Industrial Revolution.

I think one has to consider the implications of instant transmission of images by television, satellite, or film from continent to continent, and rapid transport from one part of the world to another. Sense of place is radically changing; world cities are converging in their characteristics, and world architecture too. This is a great challenge and dilemma for the architect, since although the context remains different in its grammar, traditions, structures, and materials, the real identity is being eroded.

At almost exactly the same rate, people are also trying to grab hold of some sense of continuity and self-identity through custom or tradition. The architect needs to express this need. I am not afraid of looking backwards as well as forwards. It shouldn't be an either-or situation. Hanging onto what is past is not a compromise, but a statement about reality, since 50 per cent of what makes up the present comes from the past, just as the other 50 per cent concerns what is going to happen in the future. To guess about the future of architecture is invariably a mistake. The science fiction dreams of the 1930s, for example, were wildly wrong. The images of future architecture which appeared in films and magazines can now be seen purely as an expression of the time itself, not of the future time at all, and now in the future we simply find them rather amusing period pieces.

You have experienced a steady increase in the quantity and scale of your work during a very low period for architecture in Britain and all over the world. To what do you attribute your success, and what hopes do you have for the future of architecture in Britain?

I think there is depression in Britain and America professionally because of the erosion of the traditional professional protection at the same time as there is a reduction in new projects. I think this is not altogether a bad thing. Frank Lloyd Wright deliberately stood outside the profession, although it tried very hard to seduce him back into the club. Many major modern architects, such as Lutyens, Mackintosh, Le Corbusier, Louis Kahn, or Jim Stirling have stood significantly outside the profession and if the rest of them are pessimistic that doesn't necessarily mean anything bad for architecture. The way the business of architecture is organised is being challenged today, and probably quite rightly so—it is healthier for the institution in a rapidly changing world. It is undoubtedly true that many aspects of what an architect thought was his work have been taken away from him by project managers, quantity surveyors and others. But on the other hand, I think that, as we approach the millennium, architecture is becoming increasingly recognised as the major art, and there is a much greater interest in the environment as well, not only in the green sense, but also in the sense of the context and identity of cities. By comparison, both in London and in the rest of the world, painting, sculpture and indeed music have become more moribund of late. I am very optimistic about the high game of architecture being appreciated and understood by a wider audience, and I believe the status of the creative architect is continuously improving, though changing.

Selected and Current Works

International Students Hostel

Design/Completion 1965/1968
Sussex Gardens, Paddington, London W2
International Students Club (Church of England)
Accommodation for 200 students
Conversion of existing terraced houses
Service tower: prefabricated steel core; glass fibre bathroom pods

This project was for a very low-cost conversion of six large dilapidated but historically important Victorian houses into a Church of England hostel and club rooms for 200 students. All the spaces in the old buildings were converted into student rooms, with new bathrooms and kitchens located in a service tower to the rear. The variety and character of the fine existing rooms were exploited by constructing sleeping galleries at first-floor level, and providing a multi-purpose freestanding furniture trolley which made fitted furniture unnecessary. Attic rooms were also built.

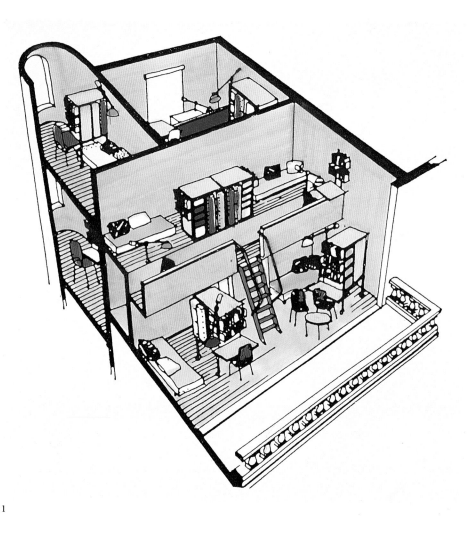

1

1   Gallery rooms on the first floor
2   Typical floor plan
3   Section through service tower
4   Student's room

16

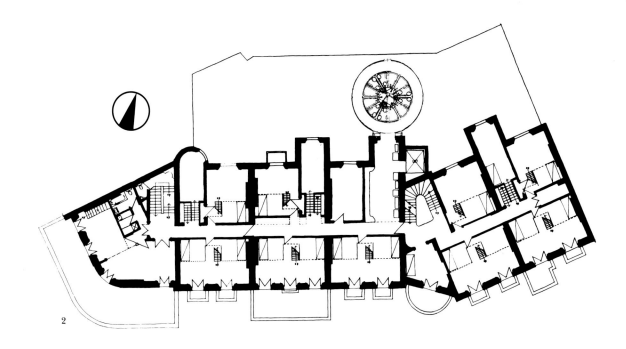

2

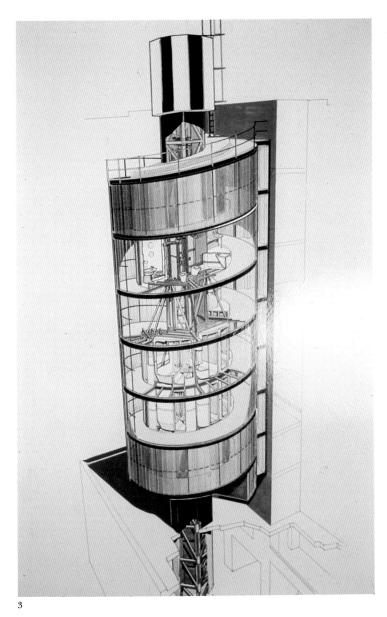

3

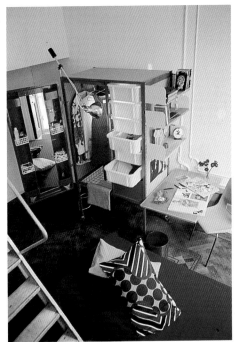

4

125 Park Road

Design/Completion 1968/1970
125 Park Road, Marylebone, London NW8
Mercury Housing Society
40,680 square feet
Steel angle frame
Corrugated anodised aluminium cladding

This low-cost project began by attempting to tailor-make 40 flats for the 40 owners who were collectively developing and living in the building. This approach was replaced by a highly flexible approach rather than a rigid one as owners' needs and personal circumstances began to vary during design and construction. Cladding is in standard, unpainted profiled aluminium sheeting; the spare concrete structure was designed by engineer Tony Hunt.

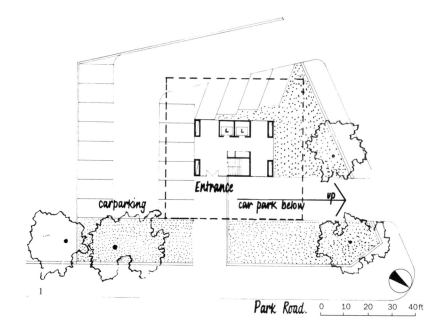

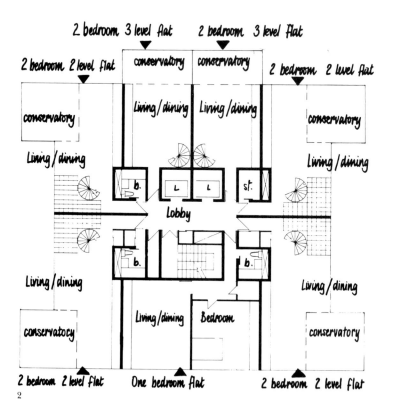

1 Site plan
2 Typical floor plan
3 Before subdivision
4 Flats as built
5 Fourteen bedsit flats
6 Two- to four-bedroom flats
7 Detail of external elevation

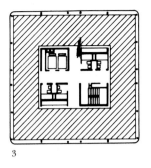

3

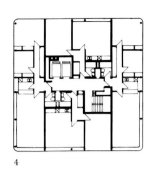

4

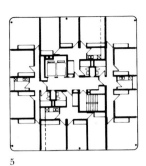

5

6

7

The Colonnades, Porchester Square

Design/Completion 1974/1976
Bishops Bridge Road, London W2
Samuel Properties Ltd
Site area: 3 acres
Reinforced concrete columns and waffle slabs
Brickwork; timber floors and roof

A three-acre urban complex of 240 dwellings, offices, shopping, pub, library (unbuilt), garden square and underground car parking, won in a limited competition. Part of the housing was formed by retaining nine large, distinctive Victorian houses and applying a new layer of living rooms at the rear in the form of a vertical sandwich. Much of the rest of the housing was on the roof-tops of the shopping precinct as linear patio houses of either 80 feet or 100 feet in length. The original mews was retained, as was the ground-level colonnade of the original houses which was extended round the newly built elements and encloses all public activities and maisonettes accessible from ground level.

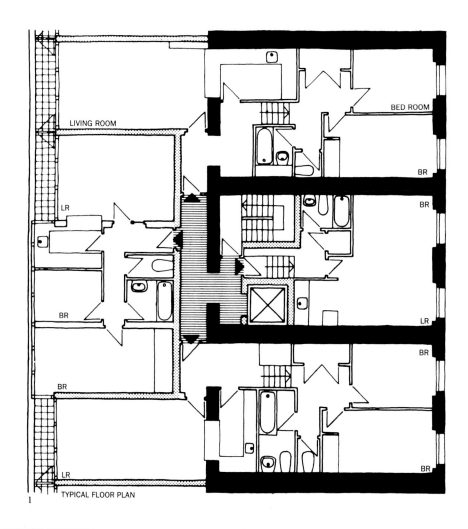

1 TYPICAL FLOOR PLAN

2

20

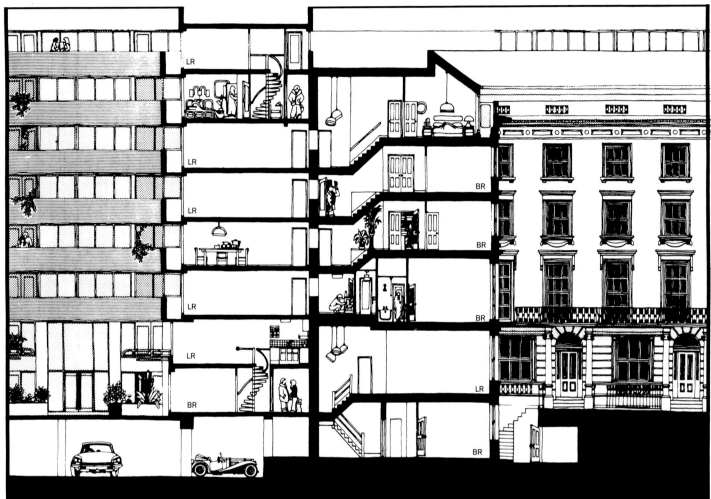

3

1 Typical floor plan
2 View from Porchester Square
3 Part section through existing buildings showing
   new rear elevations
4 Plan and sectional perspective of residential units
   above shops/offices

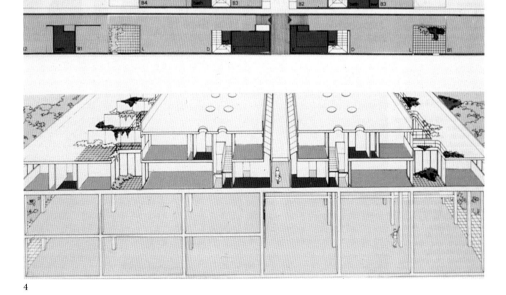

4

Oakwood Housing

Design/Completion 1978/1981
Warrington New Town
Warrington New Town Development Corporation
Approx. 350 dwellings
Timber frame
Rendered cladding timber walls; tiled roofs; precast concrete planks

The commission was to design two large adjacent housing sites in Oakwood. Houses are arranged along the lanes running north-south through the site, terminating at the retained woodland edge in a row of bollards. Each lane contains no more than 35 houses, each with its own front garden and front gate. Standardised timber frame techniques were used to economise on construction time and cost. Rather than the simple repetitive plans of the Maunsel schemes (see page 36), a concept of "universal core" (the main service, circulation, and living spaces of the house) was developed, common to all house types. Variation in size and character was then achieved by the addition of extensions in defined zones at the front and rear of each house, the aim being to encourage tenants to extend, adapt, and decorate their own house, with traditional decorative suburban elements such as trellis, porch, store and patio.

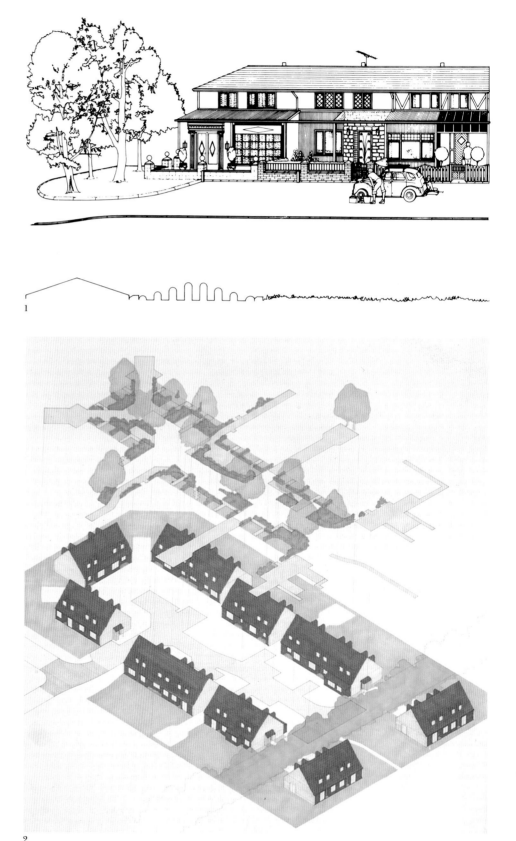

1

2

22

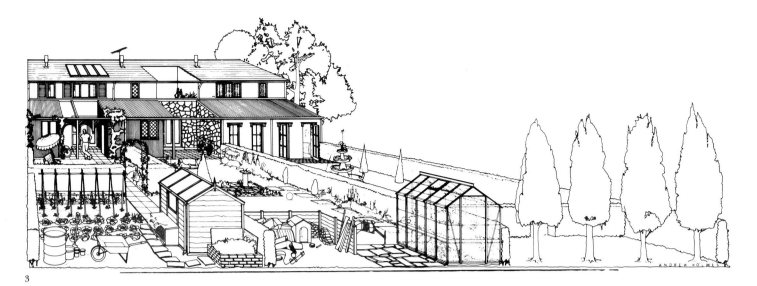

3

4

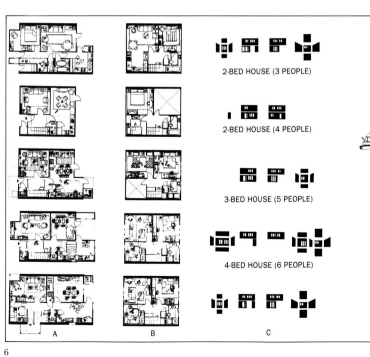

5

1 Perspective
2 Axonometric view of the lanes
3 Perspective
4 Flats and maisonettes
5 Front elevation of bungalows
6 Different house plans (A and B) result from
  adding variable timber panel add-ons (C) to
  central masonry core (D) to make range of house
  types in single terrace (E); later on management
  can vary house types (F) or tenants do their own
  add-ons (G).

2-BED HOUSE (3 PEOPLE)

2-BED HOUSE (4 PEOPLE)

3-BED HOUSE (5 PEOPLE)

4-BED HOUSE (6 PEOPLE)

A   B   C   D

E

F

G

6

Clifton Nurseries, Bayswater

Design/Completion 1979/1980
Bishops Bridge Road, London W2
Clifton Nurseries
Ground floor area: 1,800 square feet
Greenhouse area: 750 square feet
Steel frame structure
Double walled polycarbonate sheet cladding; steel frame;
thermoplastic cladding buttons

This was the first of two buildings built by Clifton Nurseries as part of their policy of revitalising vacant city sites that were temporarily derelict. Integral to the brief was the belief that the building should convey the visual pleasure of plants and gardens and be very much of the 20th century. An investigation of existing off-the-peg systems quickly revealed the necessity of starting the design from scratch. The axially organised undulating form derived from the combination of the extruded plan and the use of large sheet materials recently made available for certain types of agricultural greenhouses. Double-walled polycarbonate sheet for cladding was used for the first time in Britain, fixed to a demountable steel frame. Winter heat losses are controlled by insulation of the polycarbonate; summer heat gain is controlled by blinds on the south elevations and by a self-ventilating and heat-regulating system based on the principle of a solar chimney.

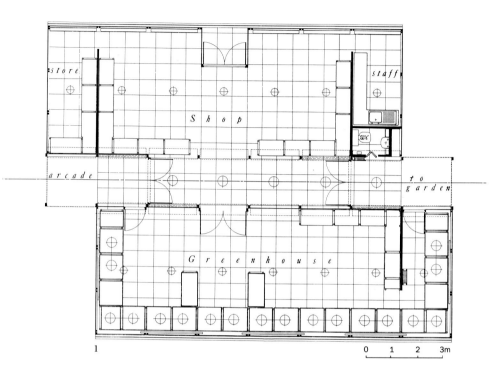

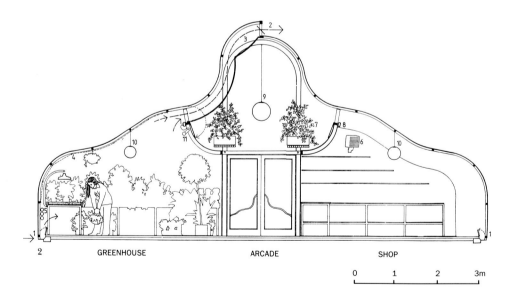

1 Floor plan
2 Cross section
3 Front elevation from Bishops Bridge Road
4 Aerial perspective
5 Construction shot showing prefabricated steelwork frame
6 Detail of entrance

24

3

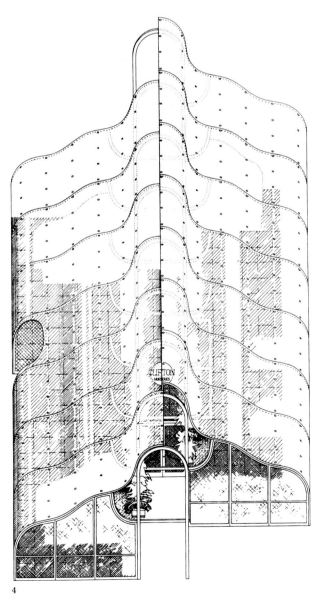

4

5

6

7 Exterior view
8 Exterior of entrance at night
9 Exterior at night
10 Interior of central arcade

7

8

9

11 Detail of the polycarbonate sheet cladding
12 Detail of the polycarbonate sheet cladding
13 Front elevation

11

12

13

Clifton Nurseries, Covent Garden

Design/Completion 1980/1981
King Street, London WC2
Clifton Nurseries
4,800 square feet
Steel frame; Teflon-coated glass fibre roof;
reinforced concrete raft
Timber walls; anodised aluminium shopfront and louvres with clear
float glass; plywood panels; four plywood columns,
two steel frame columns; postformed perspex
hollow illuminated letters

The second temporary building designed for Clifton Nurseries occupies a very prominent site owned by the Covent Garden Opera House. The architectural response combines a formal solution deriving from the surrounding streets and buildings, with an exploration of the expressive qualities of new technology. The building is aligned centrally on the axis of King Street. Since land was available on only one side of the axis, permission was obtained for the facade to be extended along a narrow strip on the other side purely as a screen, to complete the symmetry and hide car parking behind. A classical portico, based on the numerous porticos of nearby buildings, was adopted and extended in a "temple" form to become, in a light-hearted way, the underlying image of the design. The side elevation is a "rusticated" glass and timber wall. The roof is fabricated from Teflon-coated glass fibre.

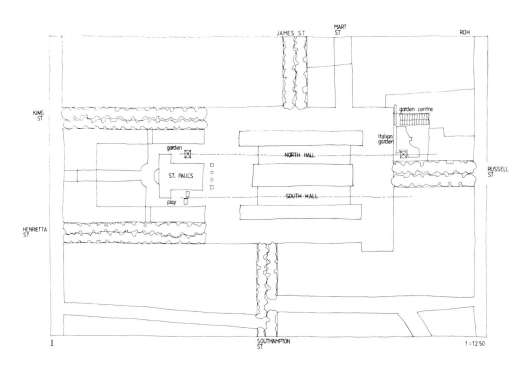

1   1 : 12 50

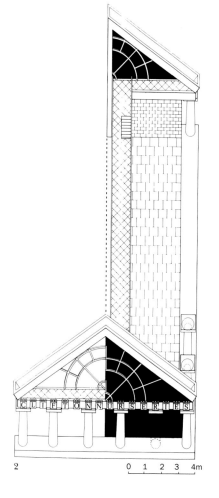

3

2   0 1 2 3 4m

4

5

7

6

1 Plan of Covent Garden
2 Vertical projection
3 View of site, as existing
4 Construction photograph showing prefabricated
   steelwork
5 Front elevation
6 Front portico elevation towards the Royal Opera
   House
7 Interior view

Clifton Nurseries, Covent Garden   31

Private House, Lansdowne Walk

Design/Completion 1979/1982
Lansdowne Walk, Holland Park, London W11
Charles Jencks and Maggie Keswick
Conversion of an existing Victorian terrace house designed together
with Charles Jencks and Maggie Keswick

The addition of a two-storey annexe, paired interlocking conservatories, a central spiral staircase and mirrored lightshaft to the existing 19th century house, among other features, created a dynamic space based on the cosmos, the solar system and the seasons. The basic grammar of the exterior has been kept or subtly altered. The interior was extensively restructured around a central circular staircase as the focus of movement. The structural cylinder, supporting both itself and the two adjacent walls, is cut at various points to allow light and surprising cross-views, sometimes uniting four rooms in a single vista. The new timber roof and ceiling structures were developed in a complex symbolic and spatial manner. The rear conservatories, with enlarged sash windows, link the interior spaces with terraces and garden: thus slots of space carry through from the street side of the house into nature.

1

1 South elevation
2 Ground-floor plan
3 First-floor plan
4 Rear elevation sketches

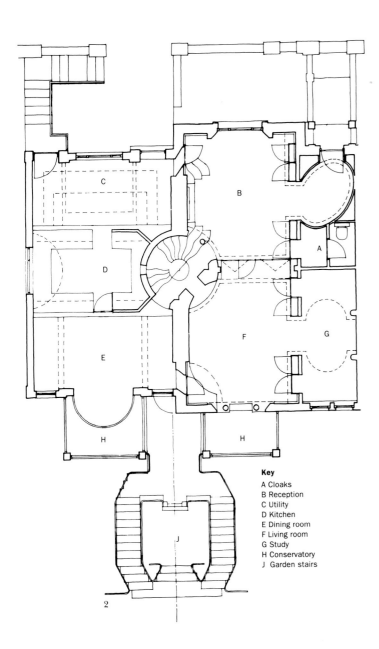

2

Key
A Cloaks
B Reception
C Utility
D Kitchen
E Dining room
F Living room
G Study
H Conservatory
J Garden stairs

Key
A Guest bedroom
B Study
C Terrace
D Master bedroom
E Dressing
F Bathroom

3

4

5 Staircase axonometric
6 Second-floor plan
7 The Sun and Light Orders, made from Runtal radiators and sconces, frame the dining area and view over the garden
8 View of the stairwell face
9 Detail of Solar staircase
10 The Moonwell
11 Detail of Sunwell

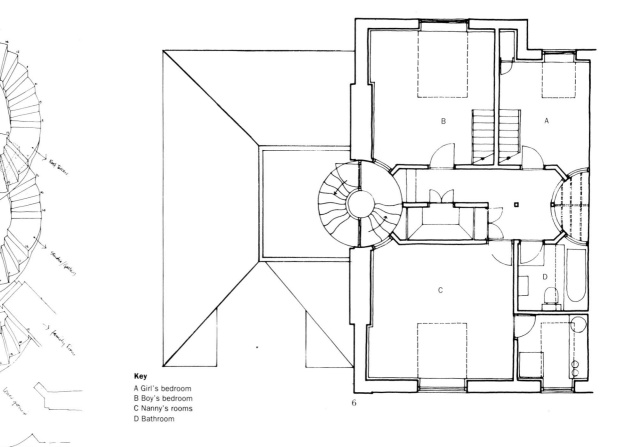

Key
A Girl's bedroom
B Boy's bedroom
C Nanny's rooms
D Bathroom

5

6

7

8

9

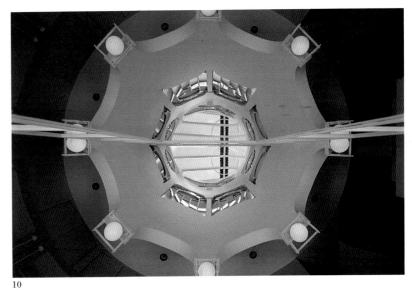

10

11

Maunsel Housing Society

Design/Completion 1972/1980
Greater London
Maunsel Housing Society
Approx. 114 dwellings
Timber frame
Brick; tile; vertical and horizontal timber boards

The commission was to design low-cost timber frame housing schemes comprising over 200 houses in all, although several of the schemes were for fewer than ten dwellings each. Dwelling types were family houses with gardens or family maisonettes over a lower-ground storey planned as a separate flat so that each dwelling had easy access to its own private garden and front door to the street. A simple repetitive plan form was developed which, like that of the London Victorian terraced house, proved to be very adaptable to different sites and constraints and to family use. The entire superstructure, roof, windows and weathering for all schemes was supplied and erected by one major timber frame manufacturer. Each project was then built under the overall control of a small local contractor so that the quality control and economies of factory-produced repetitive timber frame construction was combined with the ability to respond to each local context.

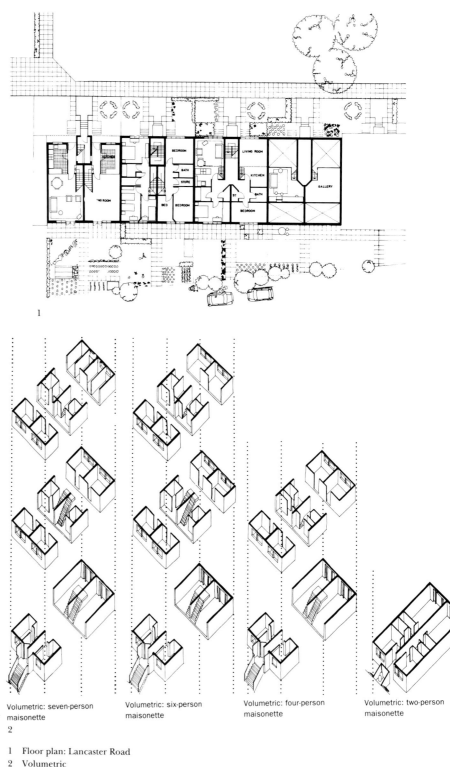

1

Volumetric: seven-person maisonette

Volumetric: six-person maisonette

Volumetric: four-person maisonette

Volumetric: two-person maisonette

2

1 Floor plan: Lancaster Road
2 Volumetric
3 Falling Lane: elevation
4 Brentwood Road, Romford: two-storey maisonettes—elevation showing face balcony
5 Claredon Road, Sutton: three-storey maisonettes—elevation

3

4

5

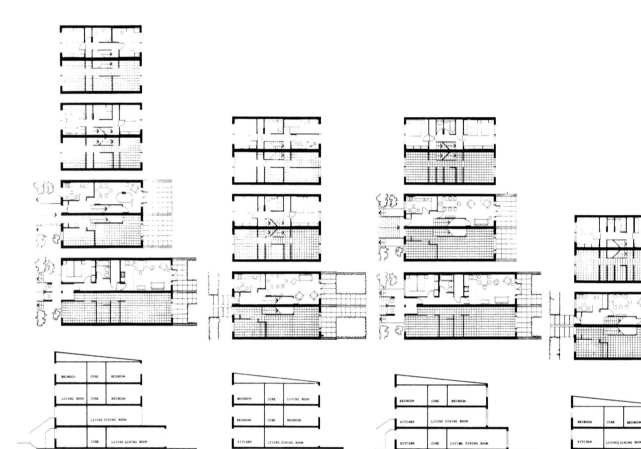

Plans and section: six-person
maisonette/two-person flat

6

Plans and section: seven-person
house

Plans and section: four-person
maisonette/two-person flat

Plans and section: four-person house

7

Urban Infill Factories, Wood Green

Design/Completion 1979/1981
Wood Green, Haringey, London N22
Samuel Properties (Developments) Ltd in partnership with London Borough of Haringey Central Area Team, funded by Plessley Pension Trust
107,500 square feet: mixed industrial and office space, comprising six units of varying sizes
Brick; steel frame curtain wall; powerfloated foundation slab
Mirrored glass; black mullions; flat felt roofs; double-glazed roof lights; standard spiral staircases with rubber treads

The commission for six factory units at Wood Green in North London was won in a developers' limited competition. A strategy of combining renovation and piecemeal redevelopment was adopted by the borough and the most run-down and least re-usable existing properties were cleared to create six sites. These were developed as a single scheme of speculative industrial units each ranging in size from the 4,300 square feet to 21,500 square feet with considerable flexibility for subdivision into different factory sizes.

A common solution was developed and adapted for each site where each building was built up to its site boundaries, whatever the plan profile, around partially enclosed courts. One of the characteristics of urban planning is that the design of open space becomes as critical as the design of the buildings themselves; at Wood Green each courtyard was a tightly designed formal arrangement of the turning circles and unloading positions of large vehicles, staff and visitor car parking, and entrance points of all vehicles and pedestrians.

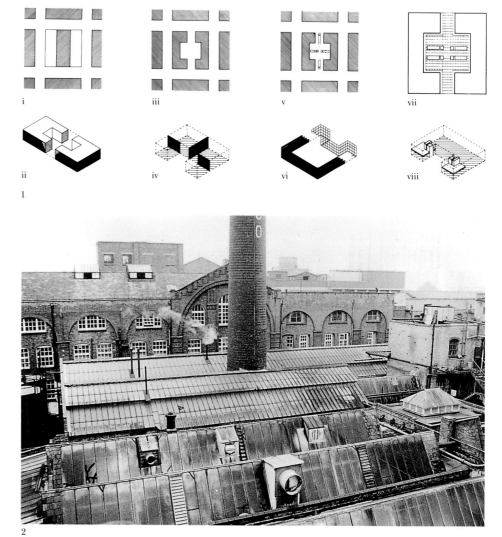

i   iii   v   vii

ii   iv   vi   viii

1

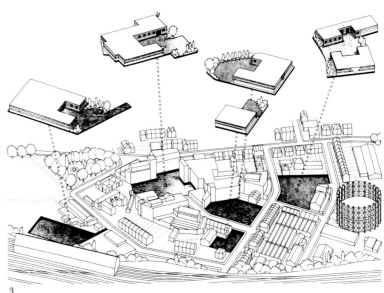

2

3

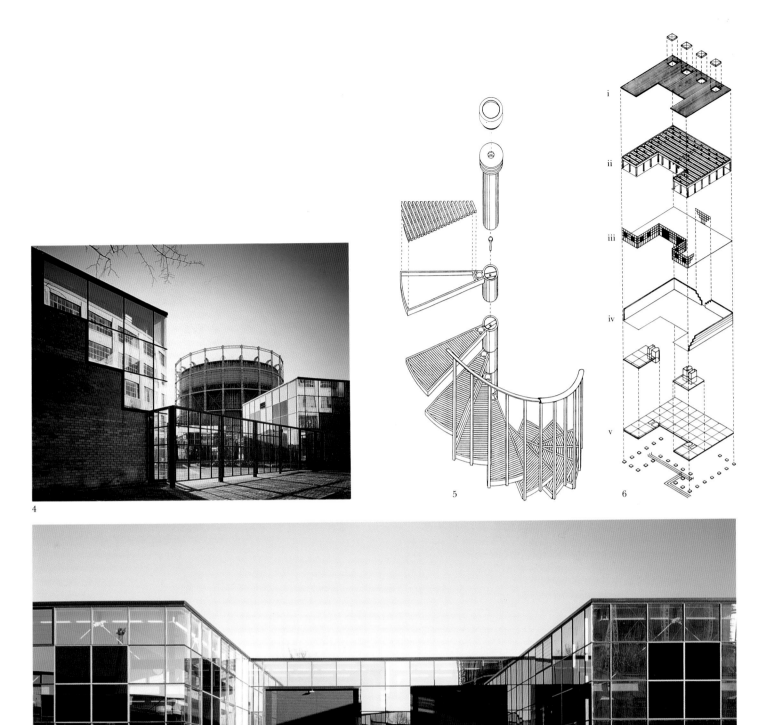

1 (i) Isolated building with no response to context; (ii) courtyard becomes the form
determinant; (iii) vehicle movement geometry establishes configuration;
(iv) four factories serviced from one courtyard; (v) two buildings;
(vi) internal subdivision to two units; (vii) two wall types; (viii) two cores
2 Existing site
3 Site plan of six courtyard buildings
4 Perimeter wall meets courtyard opening
5 The spiral staircase
6 (i) Roof covering and rooflights; (ii) steel frame structure;
(iii) internal flexible glass cladding to courtyard; (iv) exterior perimeter
brick wall and service/access cores; (v) concrete foundations and floor slab
7 Two factory enty doors flanked by office/administration wings

Crafts Council Gallery

Design/Completion 1980/1981
Waterloo Place, London WC2
The Crafts Council
7,000 square feet
Refurbishment and conversion of existing adjoining buildings
into one gallery space

The scheme for a new gallery and information centre involved conversion and extension into the adjacent building. The gallery space had to be capable of subdivision into three separate areas. Other requirements included a slide index, public information and coffee area, and office, storage, workshop and conference facilities. The ground-floor levels of the two buildings were unequal, but the mezzanine areas were the same. By re-positioning the main entrance between the two premises and lowering the level of the door and reception area, a new entry ramp was formed, which generated the main architectural strategy of the building—a central circulation axis from the entrance to the stair crossed by a cranked minor axis through the two major gallery spaces. The entrance axis orientates the public on the gallery floor and also leads them towards the staircase up to the mezzanine information centre.

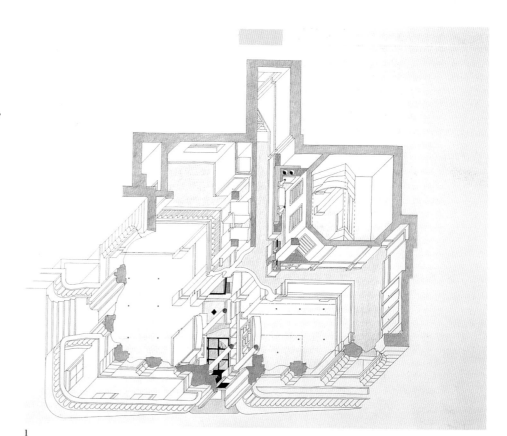

1

2

42

1 Axonometric of the three ground-floor galleries
2 Before shot of interior
3 Reception areas and front door
4 Reception area, with desk, bookshelves/display
  cabinet and fibrous plaster columns
5 Ground-floor plan
6 Gallery number one

3

4

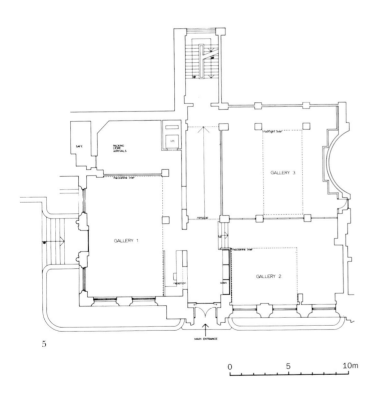

5

6

0   5   10m

7 Cross section
8 Detail of gallery three
9 Mezzanine coffee bar
10 Reception area towards new ramp and access to mezzanine

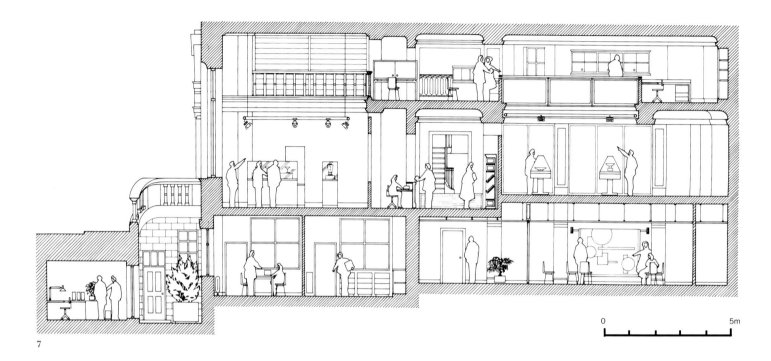

7

8

9

Alexandra Pavilion

Design/Completion 1980/1981
Alexandra Park, Haringey, London N22
London Borough of Haringey and Alexandra Palace Development Team
39,000 square feet
Shelterspan structure
Reinforced fabric panels supported and tensioned on aluminium portal frames; PVC-coated polyester; profiled metal cladding

The pavilion was constructed in 1981 as a temporary replacement for Alexandra Palace after its destruction by fire, and is still in use today. Construction is based on the standard Shelterspan system, radically adapted. PVC-coated terylene panels are supported on a rigid structure of steel portal frames. Their stable double-curved form prevents wear and tear caused by flapping in the wind. The span is 118 feet, with external purlins and diagonal rod bracing to provide longitudinal stability. The cascading appearance of the building derives from the internal organisation, consisting of a large clear-spanned hall and side aisles containing ancillary spaces. Internal climatic conditions are regulated by thermal insulation of the double fabric skin, fan-assisted natural ventilation and gas-powered heating ducted into the space through a functional "cornice" around the perimeter of the enclosure. The pavilion is designed to be demountable.

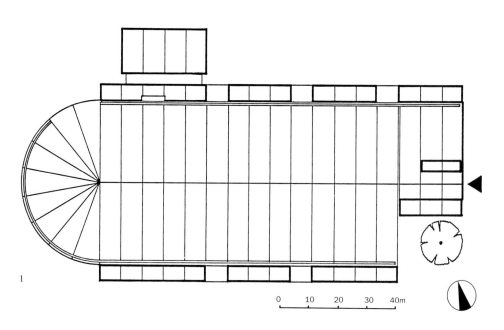

1

0   10   20   30   40m

2

1   Plan
2   Cross section/perspective view
3   Internal uplighters transform the building
    at night into a giant "lampshade"

3

Garden Festival Exhibition Building

Competition 1982 (awarded second prize)
Liverpool
Merseyside Development Corporation
90,000 square feet
Shelterspan structure
Reinforced fabric panels supported and tensioned on a steel frame;
PVC-coated polyester; profiled metal cladding

The competition brief was for a large exhibition building which could be converted into a public recreation and leisure centre at the end of the one-year Garden Festival. The design extends the thinking of the Alexandra Pavilion project: it is a fabric-covered steel-framed structure axially planned, with a large main hall and subsidiary adjacent spaces. The multiple cascading forms at the gable ends house smaller ancillary volumes, as well as reducing the scale of the building at ground level—particularly at the entrances. The single skin of PVC fabric was to be doubled in the second stage, using a superior fabric with an increased life expectancy, such as Teflon-coated glass fibre. Various colours and designs for the external envelope were explored.

1

2

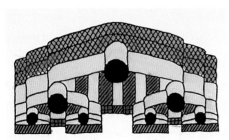

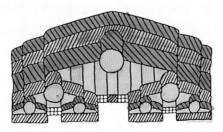

3

1 Perspective of exhibition centre
2 Plan
3 Alternative designs and colour schemes for the external envelope

Water Treatment Centre

Design/Completion 1979/1982
Reading, Berkshire
Thames Water Authority
21,500 square feet
Structural steel frame; prestressed precast concrete floors; PVC-coated
steel roof deck; plasticated PVC membrane
Curtain wall system; aluminium grid and glass panels; steel support angle;
blockwork internal walls; metal stud partitions; curved clear glass;
perforated silver and metal fixed louvres

Thames Water Authority is one of the
largest water authorities in the world,
dealing with water supply and sewage
treatment. Besides all the tank and plant
accommodation, space was needed for
laboratories, cafeterias, offices, changing
facilities, various workshops, chemical
stores, generators and general stores.
Thames Water Authority's special
knowledge and expertise is commercially
available, giving rise to large numbers of
visitors who come from all over the world
to view the methods and machinery; hence
the unusual demand for a visitors' centre.

The building arrangement combines
the visitors' centre with the everyday
operations of the water treatment plant.
Visitors are made to feel that they are at
the centre of operations, while operations
can be carried out unhindered by their
presence.

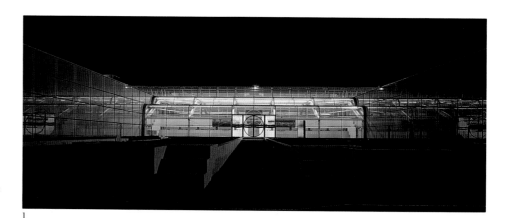

1

2

1   Main visitors' centre at night: side wings are in
    opaque blue glass
2   Visitors' gallery viewing window from the outside
3   Stores wing in foreground, offices and laboratory
    wing in distance
4   Junction of reflective glass walls and opaque glass
    "solid" cladding
5   (i) Building envelope; (ii) internal ground and
    first-floor accommodation; (iii) underground
    water treatment tanks

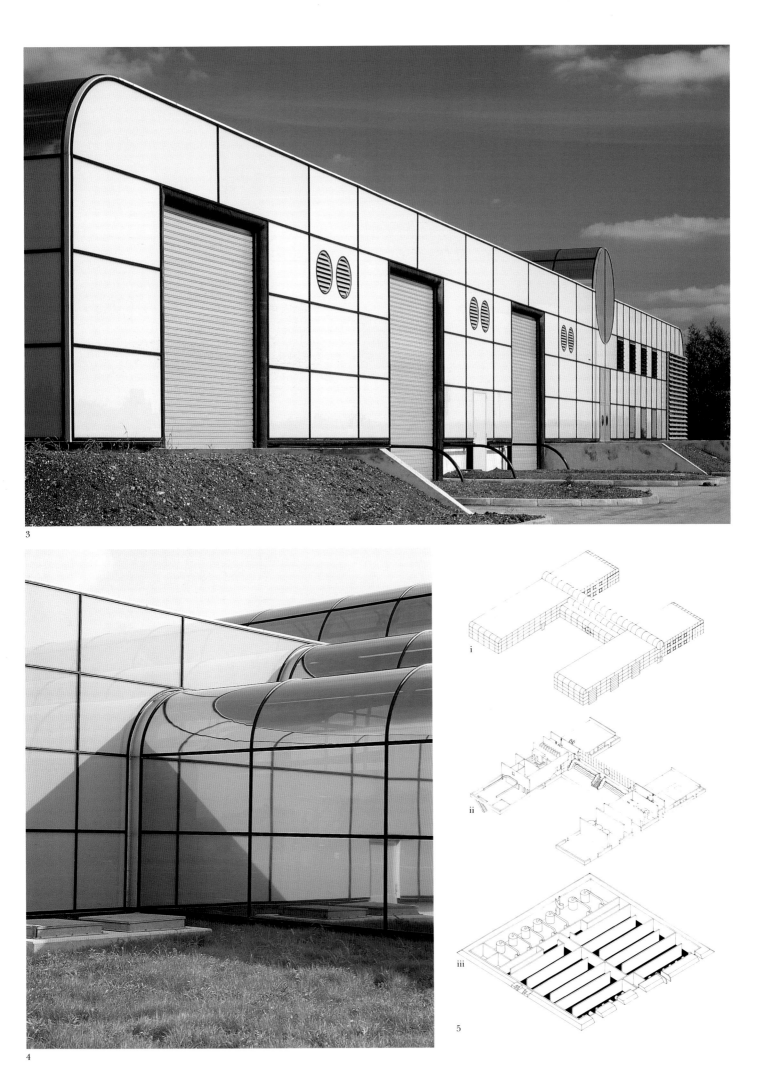

3

4

i

ii

iii

5

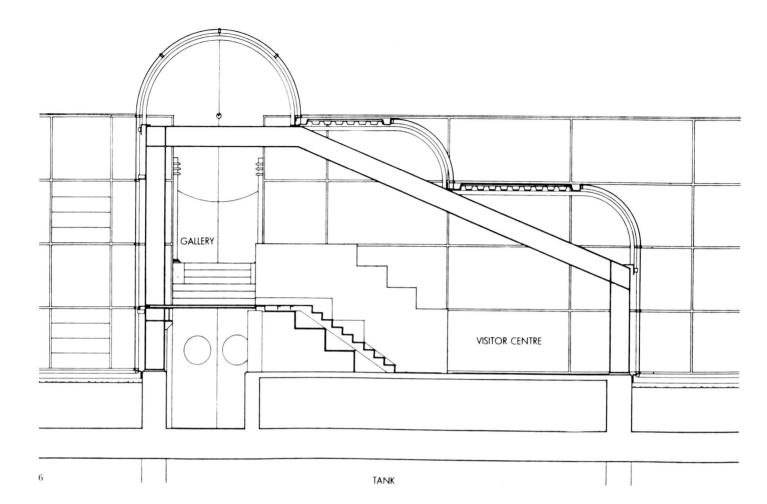

GALLERY

VISITOR CENTRE

6

TANK

7

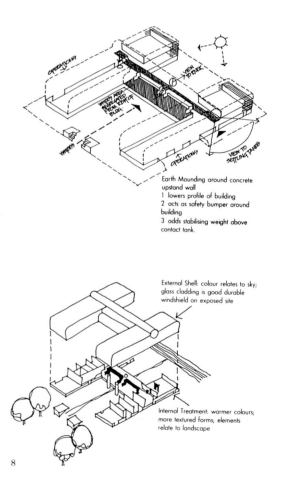

Earth Mounding around concrete upstand wall
1 lowers profile of building
2 acts as safety bumper around building
3 adds stabilising weight above contact tank.

External Shell: colour relates to sky; glass cladding is good durable windshield on exposed site

Internal Treatment: warmer colours; more textured forms; elements relate to landscape

8

6   Cross section through visitors' exhibition centre
7   Exhibition space
8   Conceptual studies
9   Interior of visitors' viewing window at the end of the gallery

9

10

10 Visitors' viewing gallery looking down to main
    exhibition space
11 Visitors' viewing gallery

11

TVam Breakfast Television Studios

Design/Completion 1981/1982
Hawley Crescent, Camden, London NW1
TVam
100,000 square feet
Part new building and part conversion of an existing 1930s industrial garage
Existing concrete structure with exposed steel monitor roof; steel portal framing in studios

Before conversion, the TVam television studios were a collection of dilapidated garages in Camden Town. The brief called for reception and hospitality areas, two television studios, control rooms, technical facilities and office space for 350 employees. The production facilities are on the ground-floor level and the administration on the first-floor level. Linking these two floors is the central stair. Sitting in a sea of blue carpet, and in the form of a Mesopotamian ziggurat, the central stair at half-floor level becomes a platform from which the activities of the first floor can be seen, and which functions as a meeting place, a sort of street corner where employees can interact. As in the great Hollywood musicals of Busby Berkeley, this stair was also regularly used as a stage set for the studio's programmes from 1983 until 1992 when the programme ceased production.

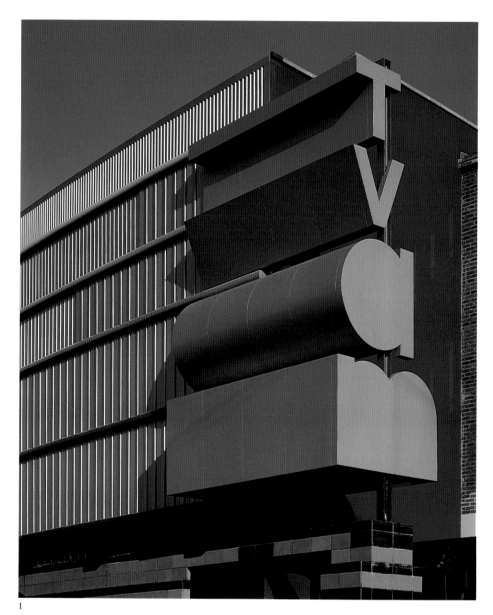

1

1   Detail of TVam logo and banded cladding
2   1930s lettering inspiration for logo
3   Canalside house with existing terraced housing
4   Canalside view
5   Ground-floor plan
6   Hawley Crescent, as existing
7   Interior of Henly's garage before conversion
8   Conceptual sketch through atrium

2

3

4

6

7

5

8

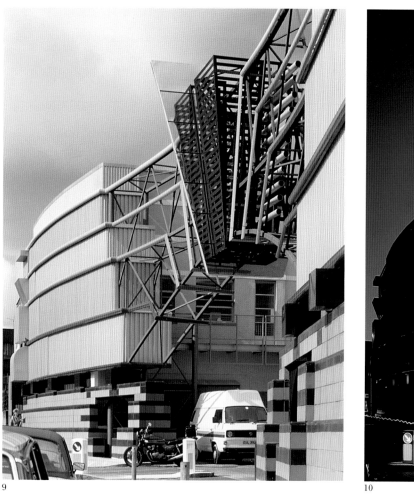

9

10

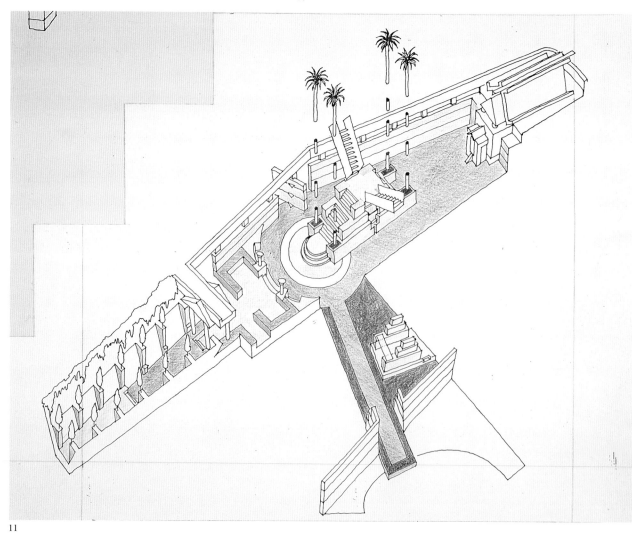

11

9 Entrance arch
10 Entrance at night
11 Axonometric of atrium
12 Exploded axonometric
13 Entrance arch and courtyard

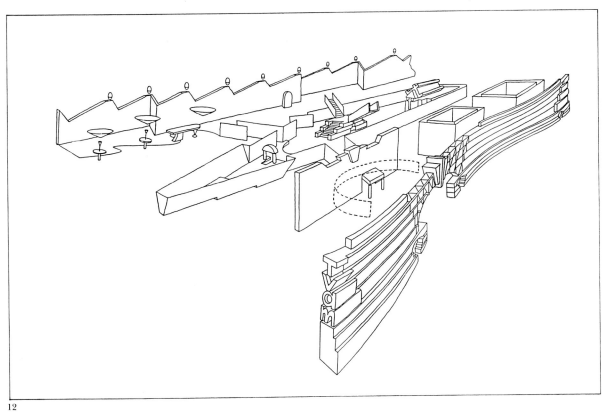

12

13

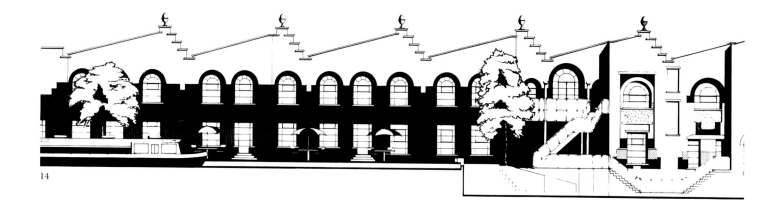

14

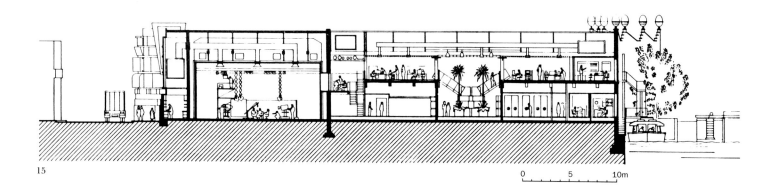

15

0 5 10m

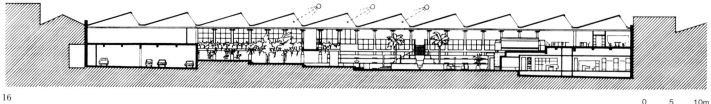

16

0 5 10m

14 Detail of canalside elevation
15 Cross section
16 Long section through full length of atrium
17 Atrium interior with transformed existing bridge
   within the Mediterranean garden

17

18

19

18 Interior of atrium
19 Detail of Mediterranean garden
20 The "eastern temple" hospitality room
21 Detail: main staircase
22 Detail of atrium
23 Detail: planters and light

20

21

22

23

24 North wall zones: (A) old brewery wall; (B) TVam
   mooring; (C) sluice/chairman's office;
   (D) terrace cafe; (E) private mooring;
   (F) the house
25 An abstracted "keystone" identifies the entrance
26 Conceptual sketch: the front wall
27 View of the hospitality room from the first floor
28 Hospitality chairs designed for TVam
29 Director's meeting table
30 Breakfast Television studio
31 Technical areas

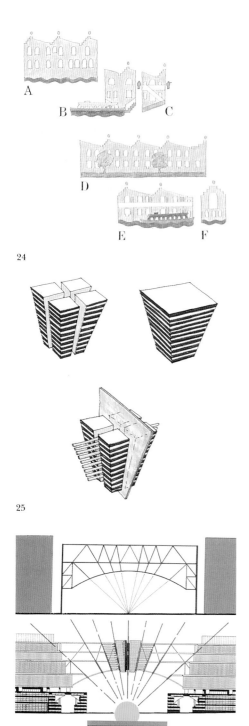

24

25

26

27

28

29

30

31

Limehouse Television Studios

Design/Completion 1982/1983
West India Docks, London E14
Limehouse Productions Ltd
79,500 square feet
Part new building and part conversion of a 1950s Banana Warehouse

This scheme comprises the conversion and extension of a 1952-built rum and banana warehouse on Canary Wharf, in the heart of London's docklands. The existing warehouse was a large three-storey brick and concrete frame building of rugged simplicity, inside which were to be inserted two television studios designed to very high technical specifications, plus ancillary production, office and workshop accommodation. A new mezzanine floor was added along the north entrance frontage to provide additional area for performers, dressing-rooms, and related facilities. At ground level a large reception area constitutes the main focus of the building, leading to the main stair and lift, the studios and production areas, and the public client rooms.

Externally, six substantial new elements were added to the entrance elevation, both to provide additional accommodation and to give the building a new identity. These are closely related in appearance and proportionate in scale to the massive bulk of the existing warehouse.

1

2

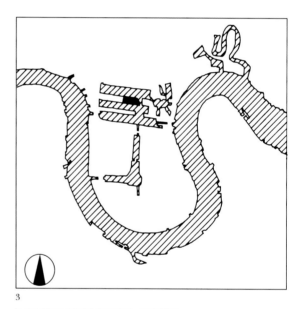

3

4

1   Existing warehouse interior
2   Existing warehouse along the dockside
3   Location plan: Isle of Dogs, 1985
4   Location plan: Canary Wharf, 1985
5   Entrance frame with projecting lobby

5

6

7

6 North facade as viewed from Billingsgate fish market
7 Front elevation detailing six add-on elements
8 Detail of front elevation
9 Ground-floor plan
10 Mezzanine-level plan
11 Part first-floor plan
12 Part second-floor plan

8

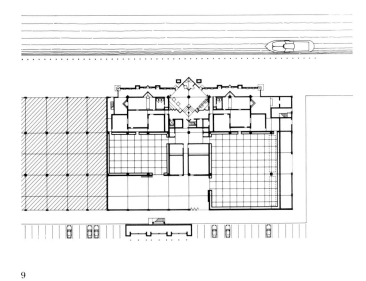

9

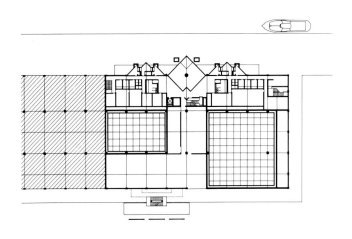

10

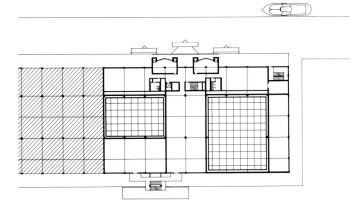

11

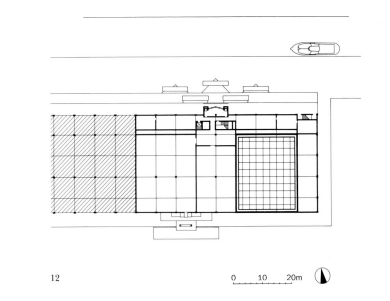

12

0   10   20m

13 Longitudinal section
14 Cross section
15 Detail of stairs and studio entrances beyond the entrance hall
16 Entrance hall
17 Entrance hall viewed from behind the reception desk
18 Conceptual sketch, balancing blocks
19 Interior of main studio

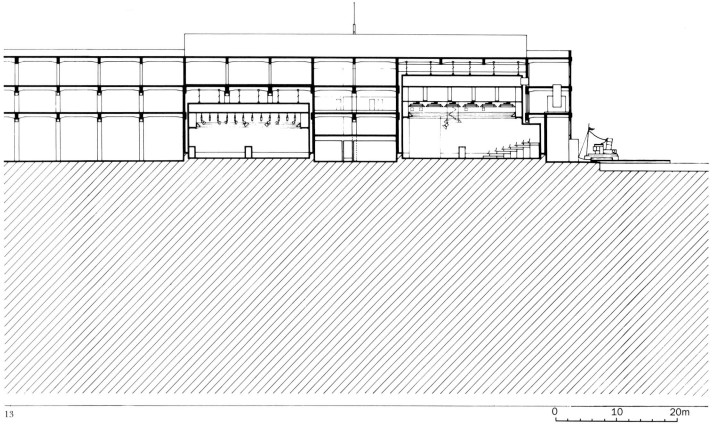

13

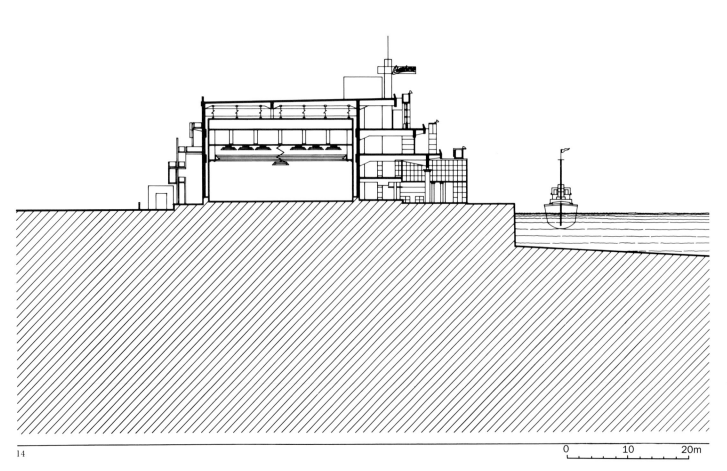

14

16

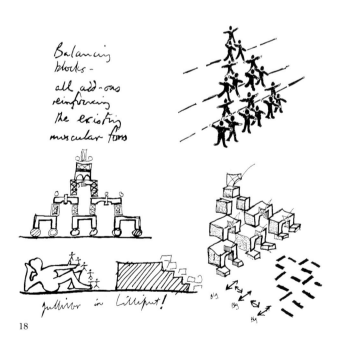

15

17

Balancing
blocks -
all add-ons
reinforcing
the existing
muscular form

Gulliver in Lilliput!

18

19

Comyn Ching Triangle

Design/Completion 1978/1985
Seven Dials, Covent Garden, London WC2
Phase 1: Comyn Ching & Company (Developments) Ltd
Phase 2: Taylor Woodrow Capital Developments
Phase 3: Finlan Properties
4,692 square feet new retail; 13,498 square feet restored retail; 11,021 square feet new office space; 14,156 square feet restored office space; 11,174 square feet residential accommodation; 7,322 square feet four townhouses plus landscaped pedestrian courtyard
Reinforced concrete columns and beams; brick plinth; brickwork; ironwork railings and window boxes; render

The Comyn Ching triangle is typical of many central urban sites—an odd-shaped plot which began as an 18th century property speculation with a mix of uses and ownerships, and developed as a complex mix of awkward geometries and substandard buildings, with most falling into single ownership.

The carefully phased scheme retained the listed buildings on the perimeter, restored their street elevations, and refurbished them for mixed-use occupation.
New corner buildings, containing office and residential accommodation, define the edges of the development. The clutter of miscellaneous infill buildings at the centre of the site was removed and replaced by a quiet, hidden courtyard, in which two new office entrances are located.

The resulting site has a clear identity, both new and restored buildings adding to the established grain of the surrounding area, and the scheme has made a significant contribution to the renewal of the Seven Dials area of Covent Garden.

1

1   Existing aerial of site
2   Exploded axonometric in context of Seven Dials, outlining corner elements
3   Existing triangle plans outlining the types of existing buildings

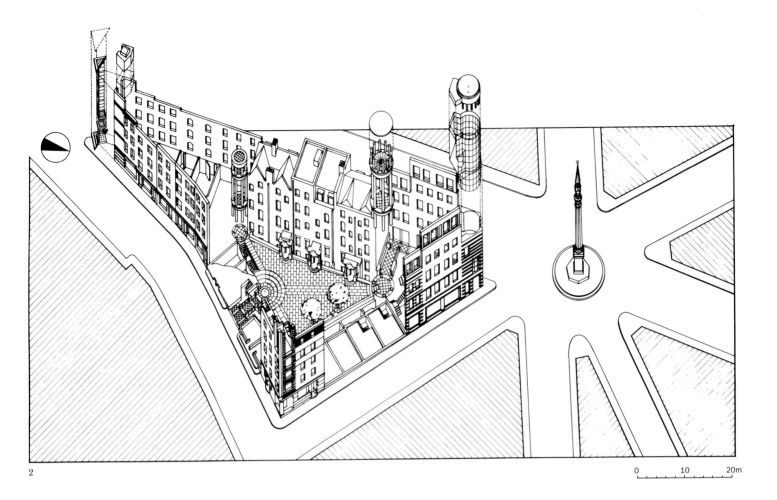

2

0   10   20m

MERCER STREET

MONMOUTH STREET

SHELTON STREET

COMYN CHING

COMMERCIAL (OTHERS)

HOUSING OVER (SUBSTANTIALLY)

OFFICES OVER (SUBSTANTIALLY)

LISTED BUILDINGS

CLOSING ORDER

3

building of poor quality
out of character with
remainder of Seven Dials

dormer workshop windows

victorian warehouse

dormer workshop windows

high

low

high

low pair

fine interior

low
pair

high
pair

fine interior

low
pair

wide
pair

narrow
pair

four similar

three low
varied

high pair

19th century tenement
building of very poor
quality, out of
scale and character
with the remainder
of Shelton and Mercer

Comyn Ching shopfront
listed grade two star

4

5

6

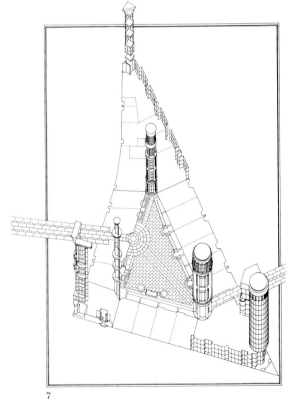

7

8

9 Detail of corner building, Shelton/Monmouth Street
10 Courtyard roof-top detail
11 Unwrapped elevations of internal courtyard
12 Detail of stonework and Lutyens seat

9

10

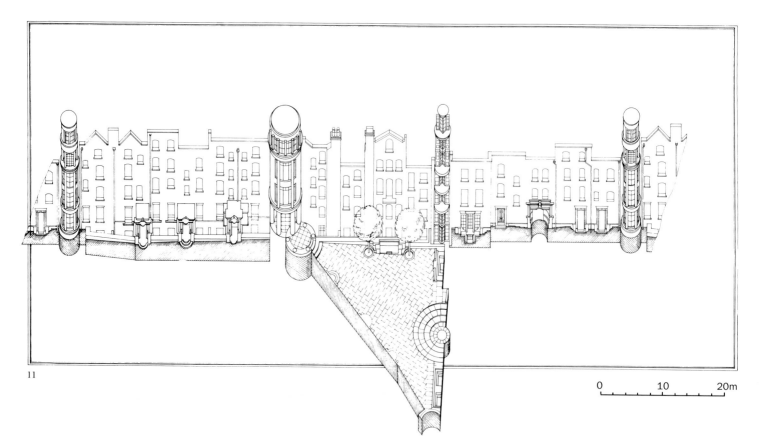

11

0   10   20m

12

Allied Irish Bank, Queen Street

Design/Completion 1982/1985
Queen Street, London EC4
Harbour Development Group
50,000 square feet
Thin-wall cladding system
Granite striations; red brick; curved glass and stainless steel canopy;
aluminium cladding; painted steel panels; polished granite; marble;
stainless steel

This infill office building in the City of London was to provide a banking hall and office accommodation on a very sensitive site in the Garlick conservation area, and close to Wren's St James' Garlickhithe Church. It is designed with two pavilion-type projecting bays at the front linked by the ground-level porch and roof-level boardroom, in order to preserve the existing rhythm of the street. The exterior is clad in pink granite with a heavy rusticated granite plinth, marking Farrell's first venture into stone, and the beginning of the move away from the glass curtain-walling which dominated new buildings in the City during the previous two decades. At the time of construction, in 1982, the thin-wall cladding system was new. Internal spaces are virtually column-free, with minimum ceiling heights to conform with St Paul's Cathedral heights requirements. Lift lobbies and cloakrooms are decorated in granite, marble and stainless steel.

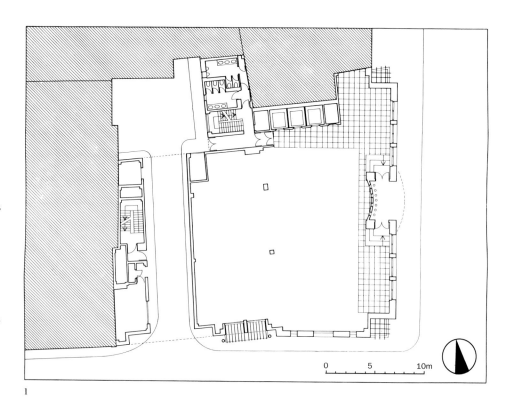

1

2

1 Ground-floor plan
2 Axonometric
3 Detail of front elevation at night
4 Granite striations turn the corner into
  Skinners Lane
5 Detail of granite striations
6 Night shot

3

4

5

6

Henley Royal Regatta Headquarters

Design/Completion 1983/1985
Henley-on-Thames, Oxfordshire
Henley Royal Regatta
15,000 square feet
Steel frame on concrete substructure
Brick; York stone; metal windows and doors; slate; metal cladding; render

The site was sensitive, adjacent to a listed 18th century bridge at the entrance to a town in greenbelt land. The brief was to house the disparate functions of the Regatta organisation in one building. River-level accommodation was required for storage of the timbers used to mark the course of the annual Regatta. These are transferred to their storage positions from a central wet dock, which penetrates almost the full length of the building and constitutes the key organising axial spine. The main level contains offices, storage and reception spaces, and a double-height committee room, with a balcony, which commands magnificent views over the River Thames, as does the Secretary's flat in the roof space.

The architectural conception was a formal, even "civic", building, given the importance of the Regatta in the life of Henley, combining the influence of English building traditions and the typology of the Thames boathouse with that of the Venice Arsenale.

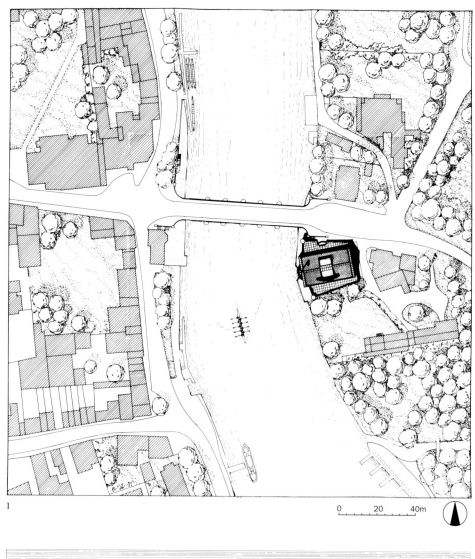

1

0   20   40m

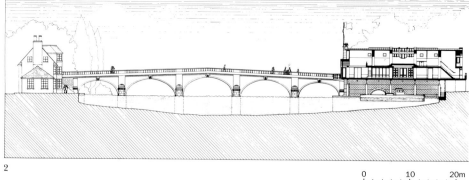

2

0   10   20m

1 Roof plan in context
2 Longitudinal section and elevation of bridge looking north
3 View along the River Thames
4 Three sections through the boathouse
5 River elevation
6 Henley Royal Regatta boathouse as existing

3

5

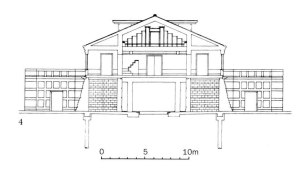

4

0   5   10m

6

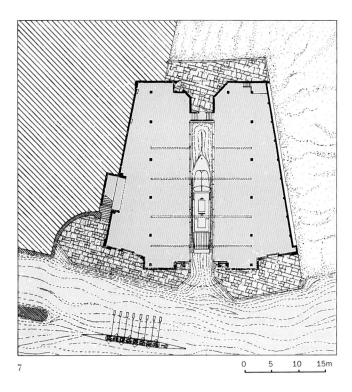

7

0 5 10 15m

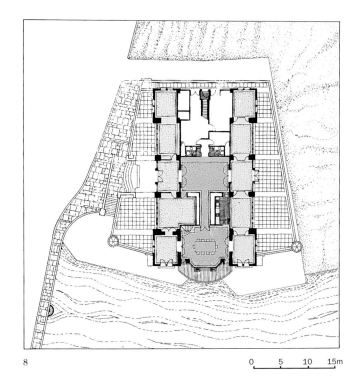

8

0 5 10 15m

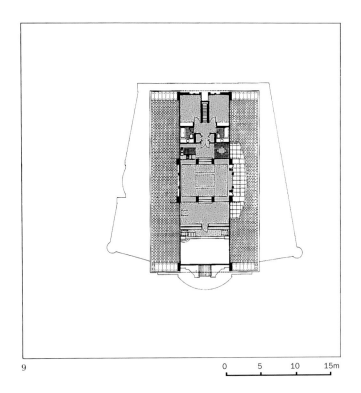

9

0 5 10 15m

10

7 River-level plan
8 First-floor plan
9 Second-floor plan
10 Vertical projection
11 Interior of accommodation on the second floor
12 Conference room with view over the River Thames
13 Front elevation at night

11

12

13

Temple Island

Design/Completion 1988/1991
Henley-on-Thames, Oxfordshire
Henley Royal Regatta
2,500 square feet
Main building: Loadbearing masonry
Balcony: Mild steel frame
Painted render; painted cast iron and mild steel

Designed as a neo-classical folly in 1771 by James Wyatt, the Temple is a well-known and well-loved landmark on this reach of the River Thames. Following the commission for its new headquarters building, Terry Farrell was asked by Henley Royal Regatta to design a balcony and staircase for this fine historic building as part of a comprehensive programme of restoration. Most of a decayed 19th century timber balcony was restored using a lightweight metal construction. The symmetry and classical language which influence the form and detailing of the structure respond to the character of the original Wyatt building.

The new balcony and stair provide access from the garden to the Etruscan Room and the belvedere above, affording magnificent views of the river, and of course the annual Henley Regatta itself.

14

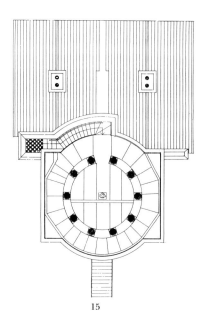

15

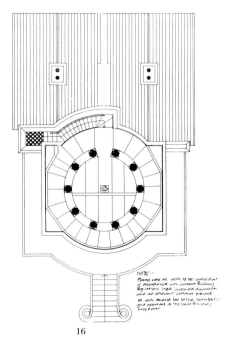

16

17

18

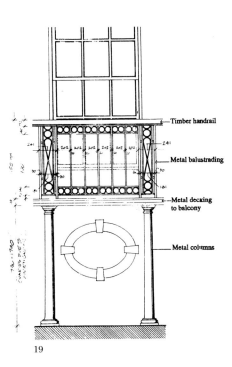

19

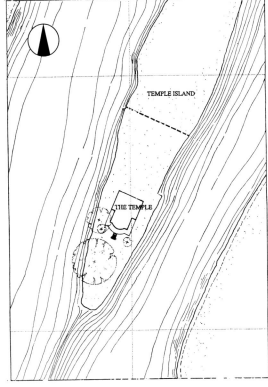

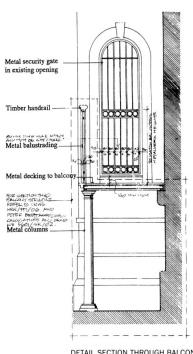

Metal security gate
in existing opening

Timber handrail

Metal balustrading

Metal decking to balcony

Metal columns

DETAIL SECTION THROUGH BALCONY
AND ELEVATION OF SECURITY GATE
SCALE 1:20

Midland Bank, Fenchurch Street

Design/Completion 1983/1986
95-97 Fenchurch Street, London EC3
Central & City Properties
45,000 square feet
Steel frame structure; in situ concrete slabs on proprietary metal decking
Basement: Reinforced concrete; retaining walls
Colour coated metal cladding; pink flame textured granite cladding;
polished grey granite cladding; granite plugs; aluminium framework;
polyester powder-coated double glazed windows

This office and banking building on an exceptionally prominent corner site provides a fully serviced and air-conditioned environment capable of accommodating new and future office technology. The building is conceived as a "gateway" to the City, with a distinctive corner tower.

While construction techniques are contemporary, the image and substance of the building are in character with the fine adjacent buildings on Leadenhall and Fenchurch Streets. Cornice lines from the adjacent building have been continued and, together with street-level rustication, serve to articulate the scale. The tower on the corner at St Michael's Well has a circular colonnaded portico at ground level, forming the entrance to the bank.

The treatment of the external facade is in two different granites. The upper levels of the building, set back progressively above the main cornice level, are clad in metal and glass curtain walling to suggest a traditional attic or roof structure.

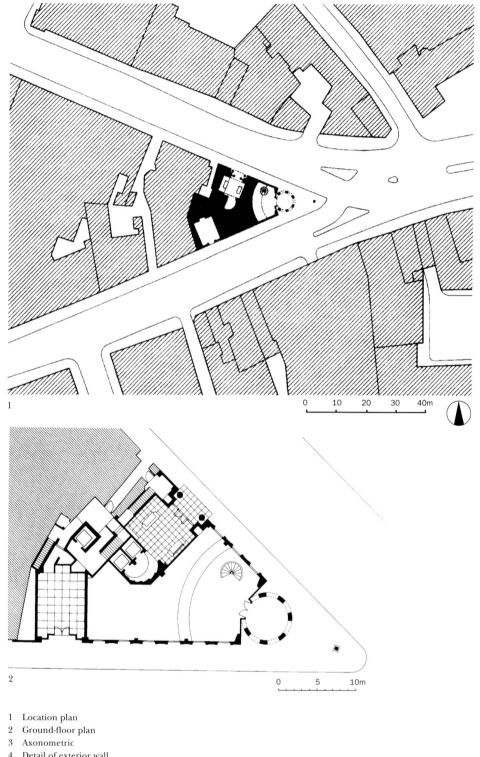

1

0   10   20   30   40m

2

0   5   10m

1   Location plan
2   Ground-floor plan
3   Axonometric
4   Detail of exterior wall
5   "Before" shot of site
6   Detail of doorway canopy
7   (i) Location diagram; (ii) corner column;
    (iii) perspective; (iv) ground-level elements;
    (v) roof-top elements

3

4

5

6

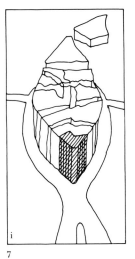

i

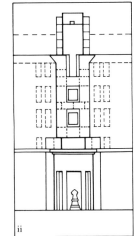

ii

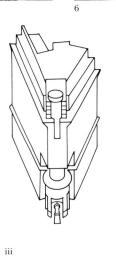

iii

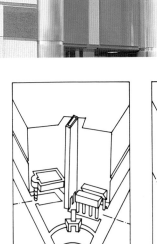

iv

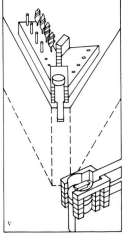

v

7

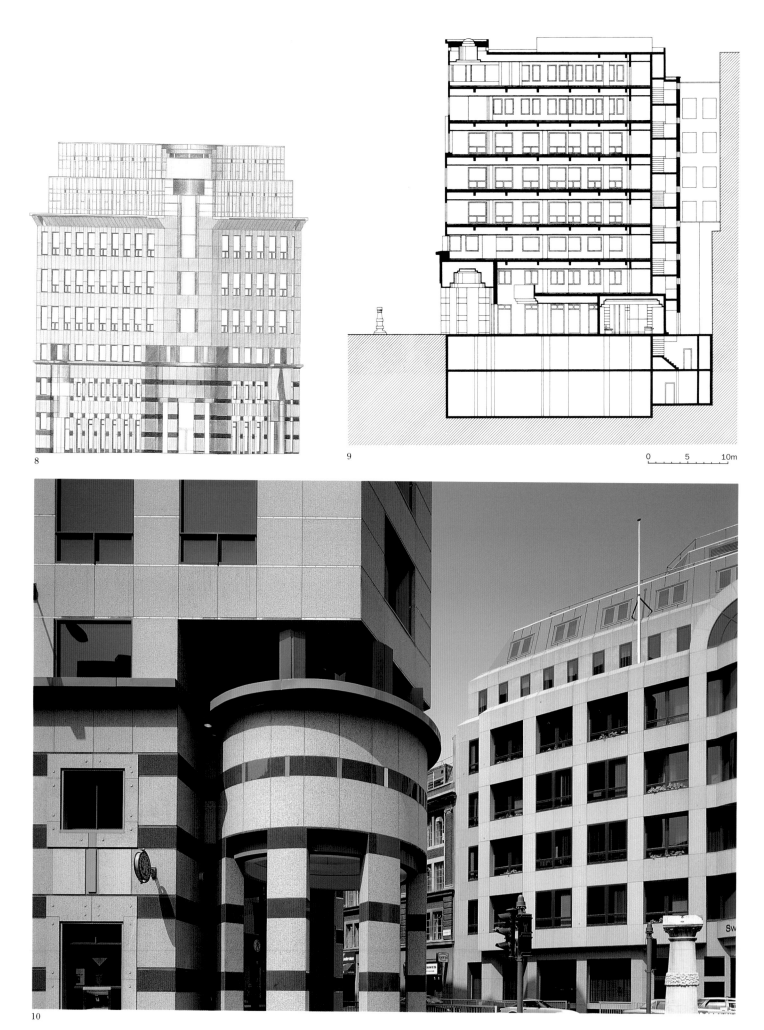

8

9

0   5   10m

10

11

12

13

King's Cross Master Plan

Design/Completion 1987
London NW1
Master plan study for British Rail
6,101,100 square feet (offices); 3,309,100 square feet (residential
accommodation); 620,280 square feet (retail and commercial leisure
facilities); 331,100 square feet (industrial); 162,670 square feet
(public facilities); 118,400 square feet (British Rail)

The master plan study accommodates
6 million square feet of offices, leisure,
residential, retail, transport and
community uses, including interchanges
for the Channel Tunnel, on 125 acres of
largely derelict British Rail land between
King's Cross and St Pancras stations.
It is centred around the canal, superseded
by the railways in the last century.
The associated architectural heritage
is preserved and revitalised, approached
from the main road by a new boulevard.
Pedestrian, cycle and vehicular routes are
mainly at ground level while interchanges
for the Channel Tunnel terminal are
provided both at ground and below-
ground levels. The existing rail and
underground complexes are improved
and better integrated with other uses.
The proposals were intended to
make a significant addition to London's
townscape, relating to the surrounding
area in a neighbourly, sensitive and
appropriate manner, and allowing
a variety of architectural forms
to be incrementally accommodated,
following traditional patterns of urban
change and development.

1

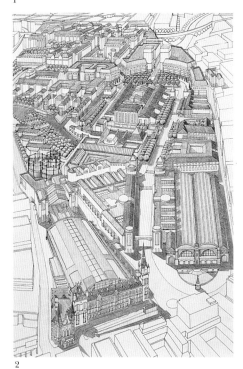

2

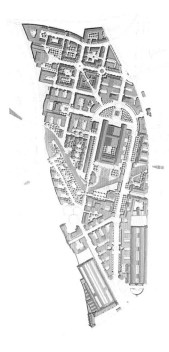

3

1   King's Cross, as existing
2   Aerial perspective
3   Master plan
4   The plan: context and urban design
5   The plan: uses and communications
6   Residential uses
7   Community and public spaces
8   Office, retail and commercial areas

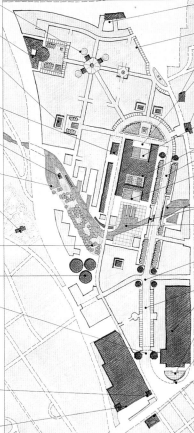
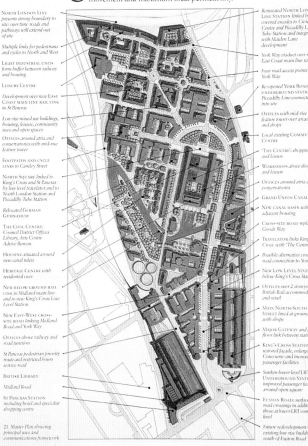

movement and maximum local permeability.

Housing enclosing residents' private squares with corner shops

Leisure Centre with local shops and public square as focus for residents

Four mid-rise towers of business use with penthouse roof tops rising to 12-13 storeys, are the only buildings in the scheme above 8 storeys

1864 German Gymnasium building with fine roof structure relocated as part of civic complex

Restored listed Lock Keeper's Cottage and existing Canal Basin

Major environmental improvements to canal to form an ecological corridor and recreation centre

Ancient site c600 AD of St Pancras Church. Present 1350 building with well tree'd graveyard

Preserved and protected Camley Street Natural Park

1834 Historic decorated Gas Holders, retained and restored

The plan suggests the removal of the Great Northern Hotel and one listed gas holder to give a wide and impressive approach to the new arcaded street and giving functional and visual access to the site. If the removal of the hotel is not achieved, the access can be modified accordingly

St Pancras Gothic Landmark Tower on axis with gateway entrance to New King's Cross

1868 Sir George Gilbert Scott's existing Gothic St Pancras Station restored

1887-1917 Reinstated Maiden Lane Station with paved square to forecourt with small shops

Arcaded Link from railway station to tube station along York Way

Re-opened Edwardian tiled Underground Station

New Square surrounded by civic buildings, shopping and arcades

Imposing and attractive Edwardian school building visually linked to centre of New King's Cross

Formal Civic Centre, set between existing wings of Cubitt's granary

'The Centre'

Generous tree-lined wide Avenue

1851 Handsome Cubitt Granary, refurbished and re-establishing access for boats to Regents Canal forming Heritage Centre

Covered arcaded 'Palladian' Pedestrian Bridges

South Square with re-opened canal basin with pedestrian promenades surrounded by shops and housing

Tower elements mark major change in streets and link the scheme's three main public street forms

Arcaded Main Street

Cubitt's 1852 existing engineering masterpiece: King's Cross Station

New public square at King's Cross with sunken space opening up underground station area

Recreated Monument of King's Cross to George IV 1830

Existing Camden Borough Council Offices linked at ground, lower ground and upper levels across Euston Road to stations and New King's Cross square

22 Master Plan showing massing, townscape and landscape. Important long and short distance views are unimpaired

North London Line presents strong boundary to site: over time roads and pathways will extend out of site

Multiple links for pedestrians and cycles to North and West

Light industrial units form buffer between railway and housing

Leisure Centre

Development over new East Coast main line rail link to St Pancras

Low rise mixed use buildings, housing, leisure, community uses and open spaces

Offices around atria and conservatories with mid-rise feature tower

Footpaths and cycle links to Camley Street

North Square linked to King's Cross and St Pancras by low level travelator and to North London Station and Piccadilly Tube Station

Relocated German Gymnasium

The Civic Centre: Council District Offices Library, Arts Centre Advice Bureau

Housing situated around new canal inlets

Heritage Centre with residential over

New below ground rail link to Midland main line and to new King's Cross Low Level Station

New East-West cross-site road linking Midland Road and York Way

Offices above railway and road junction

British Library

Midland Road

St Pancras Station including hotel and specialist shopping centre

21 Master Plan showing principal uses and communications framework

Reinstated North London Line Station linked by covered arcades to Civic Centre and Piccadilly Line Tube Station and integrated with Maiden Lane development

York Way viaduct over new East Coast main line rail link

Four road access points to York Way

Re-opened York Road Underground Station on Piccadilly Line connected into site

Offices with mid-rise feature tower over arcades and shops

Local existing Community Centre

'The Centre': shopping and leisure

Workshops above shopping and leisure

Offices around atria and conservatories

Grand Union Canal

New canal basin with adjacent housing

Cross-site road replacing Goods Way

Travelator links King's Cross with 'The Centre'

Possible alternative cross-site road connection to York Way

New Low Level Station below King's Cross Station

Offices over 2 storeys British Rail accommodation and retail

Main North-South Street lined at ground level with shops

Major Gateway and first floor link between stations

King's Cross Station with restored façade, enlarged Concourse and increased passenger facilities

Sunken lower level LRT Underground Station improved passenger facilities around open space

Euston Road surface level road crossings in addition to those at lower LRT concourse level

Future redevelopment of existing low rise buildings to south of Euston Road

4

5

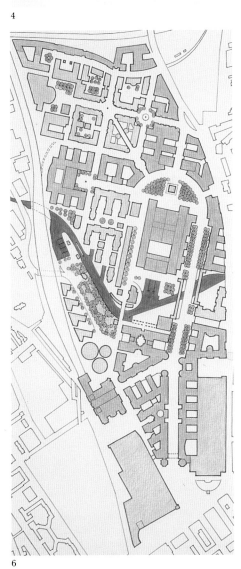

6

7

8

Tobacco Dock

Design/Completion 1985/1990
Pennington Street, Wapping, London E1
Tobacco Dock Developments Ltd
160,000 square feet
Slated hipped roof structure is supported by branching cast iron stanchions; brick groin vaulting on granite columns; timber piles and brick footings
Lantern King post truss and braces; cast iron crown piece and diagonal braces; Queen post truss; patent glazing rooflights; glazed walling; brick vaults; York stone paving

This project comprised the restoration and conversion of a significant historic Grade 1 listed dockside building dating from 1806, representing part of the original early 19th century expansion of London docks. The design of the internal structure as a prefabricated system of standard parts was unique. The building had six bays, each spanning 54 feet with a clearance height of 12 feet 6 inches. The first part of the project was the restoration of the original building fabric, involving careful repair and the replacement of missing sections of the warehouse structure with fragments of the same type of structure from buildings on adjoining sites which were threatened with destruction. The second part was the careful insertion of shopping and entertainment facilities into the restored historic fabric, including the rebuilding of the original dockside. Shops are organised around two main open courts on two floors. The removal of the roof and skin floor provides natural light and ventilation to the vaults below.

1

2

1   Dockside elevation
2   Aerial photograph of Tobacco Dock
3   Evolution of plan over time
4   Roof plan in context
5   Existing warehouse buildings
6   Detail of column

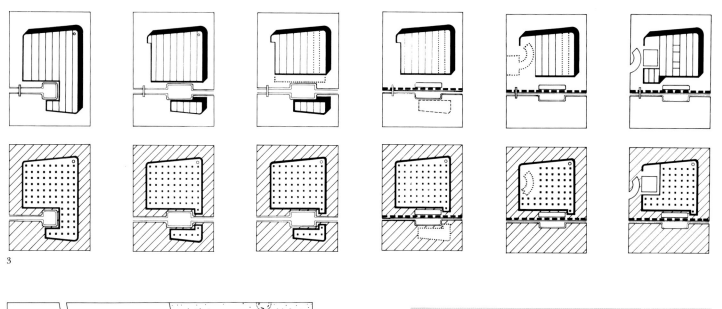

3

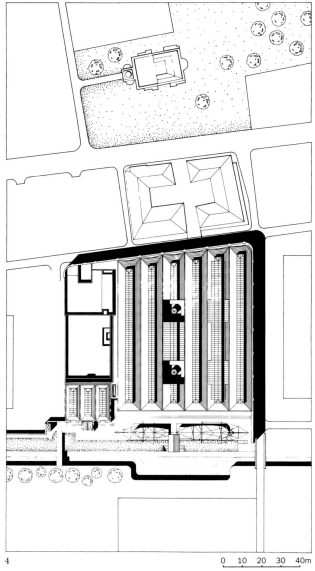

4

0   10 20 30 40m

5

6

7

8

9

10

0   10   20m

7 North elevation
8 West elevation
9 South elevation
10 East elevation
11 Vault-level plan
12 Skin-floor plan in context

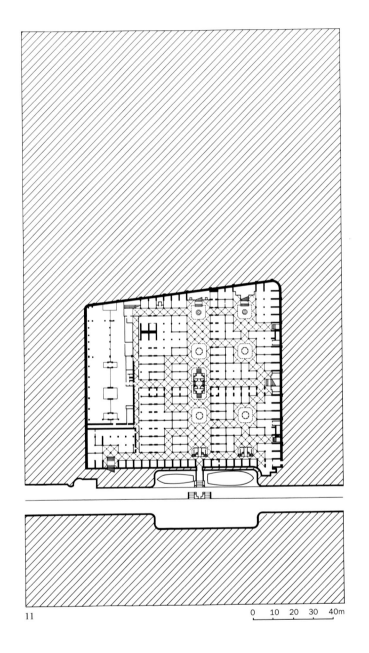

11

0 10 20 30 40m

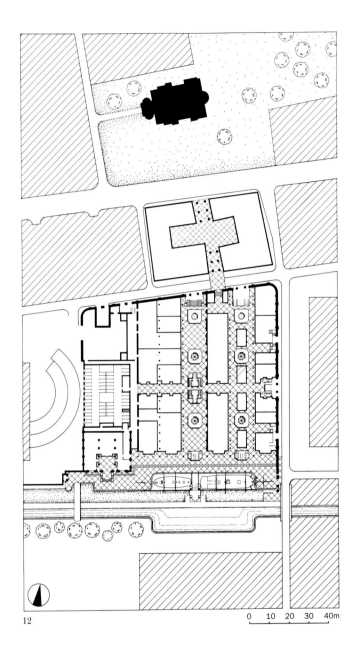

12

0 10 20 30 40m

13 Existing warehouse buildings
14 East elevation, dockside entrance
15 Pennington Street entrance at night
16 Open courtyard

13

14

15

17

18

19

17 Existing vaults
18 Detail of vault-level shopfronts
19 Vault level
20 Vault-level shopfront
21 Pencil drawing of arched entrance elevation
22 Detail of keystone

20

21

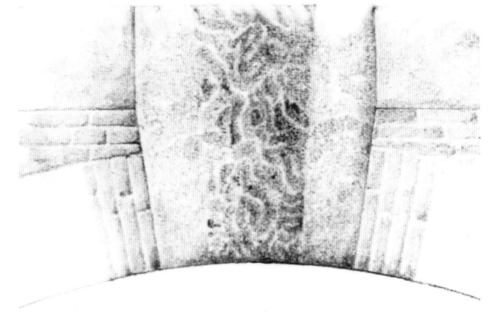

22

23

24

25

23 Detail of balustrade
24 Detail of stair balustrade
25 Interior of shop, skin-floor level
26 Restaurant entrance, skin-floor level

26

27 Detail of shopfronts, skin-floor level
28 Detail of shopfronts, skin-floor level
29 Shops on skin-floor level
30 Skin-floor level

27

28

29

Embankment Place

Design/Completion 1987/1990
1 Embankment Place, Villiers Street, London WC2
Greycoat PLC
625,000 square feet
Nine bowstring steel arches on hand-dug caissons; suspended
concrete floors on metal decking
Aluminium framed curtain walling with polished and frame textured granite
facings; three-dimensionally curved metal cladding to arches; brick;
architectural masonry; profiled metal curved roof; membrane roofs

The primary development at Embankment
Place is a new office building, occupying
the air rights space above Charing Cross
Station. It is technologically innovative,
involving suspension of seven to nine
storeys of offices above the railway tracks,
to isolate the space from railway vibration.
The resulting bowstring arch over the
tracks, supported on 18 columns rising
through the platforms, frames a new
waterfront landmark at this critical point
on the River Thames.

Environmental improvements included
in the master plan had a significant impact
on the surrounding area, notably
Villiers Street and Embankment Place,
Embankment Gardens (including
restoration and an improved setting
for York Watergate), and the station
concourse and forecourt. Hungerford
Bridge was extended to Villiers Street
and onto the station concourse, providing
a direct route to the South Bank Arts
Centre on the other side of the river.

In order to make the scheme legible
both from a distance and close up, design
details in the master plan were carried
through to cladding and finishes.

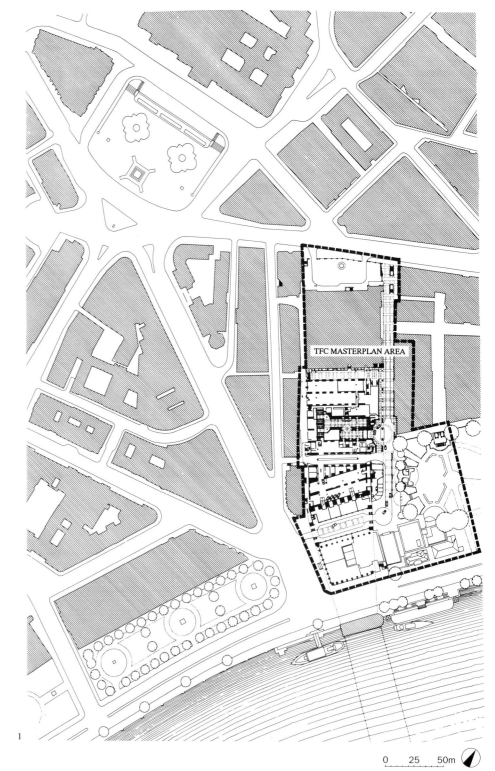

1

0   25   50m

2

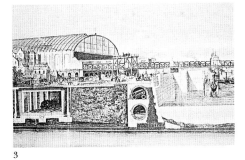

3

4

5

6

1   Master plan area highlighted
2   Perspective view from the South Bank
3   Cross section of the Embankment at Charing Cross, 1863
4   Conceptual sketch
5   Aerial view over the River Thames looking east
6   Aerial view facing north-west towards Trafalgar Square

7   Level two plan
8   Level seven plan
9   Typical office floor plan
10 Projected axonometric view
11 River elevation/section through station and retail
12 Night view from across the River Thames

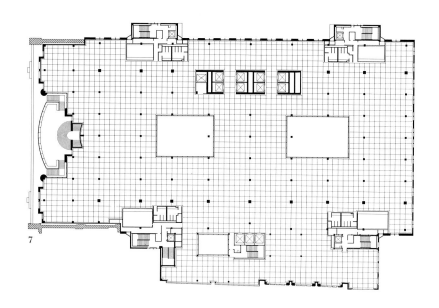

7

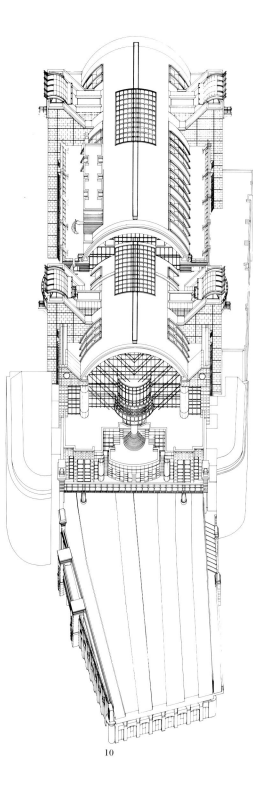

10

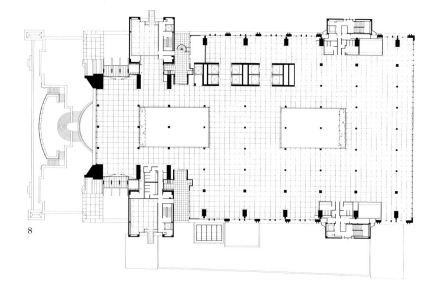

8

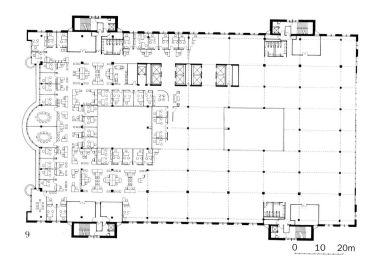

9

0   10   20m

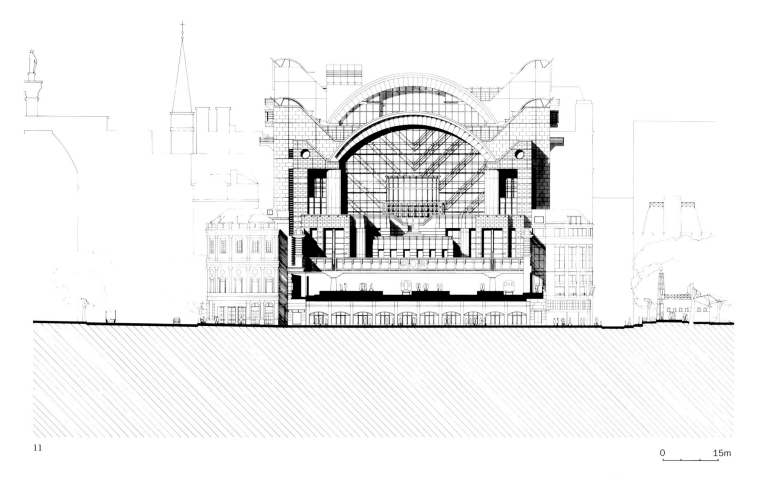

11

0   15m

12

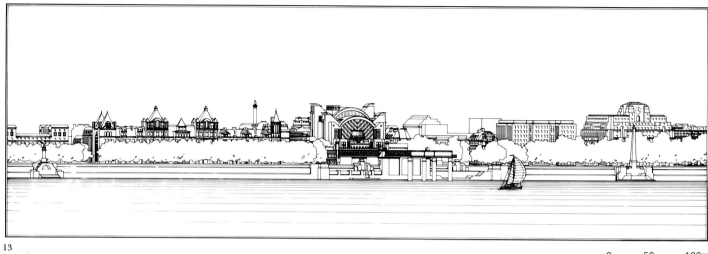

13

0   50   100m

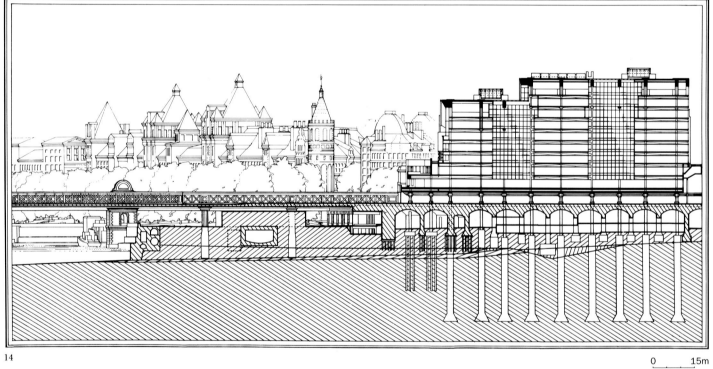

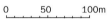

14

0   15m

15

16

17

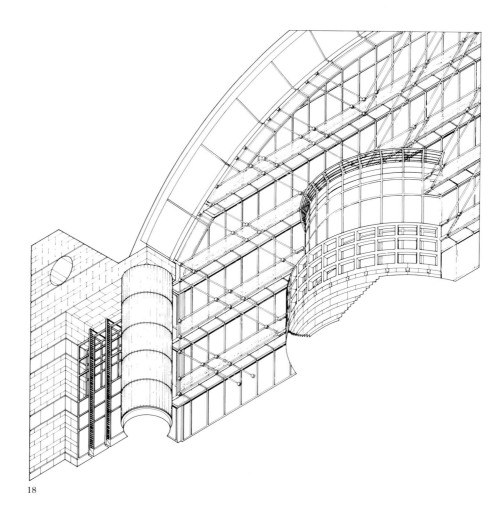

18

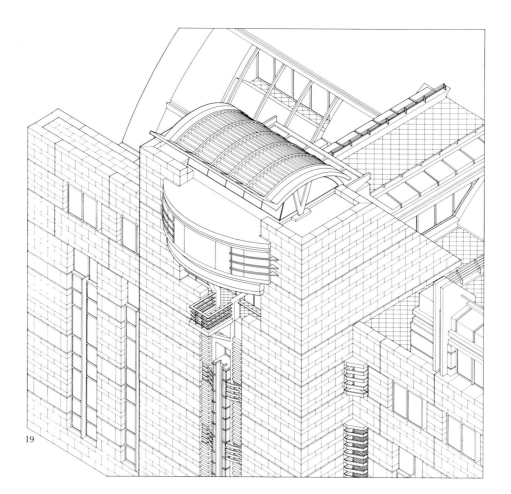

19

18 Isometric view, detail of river elevation
19 Isometric view of core tower
20 Bow window to river facade

20

21

22

23

24

25

26

27

28

29

30

31

29 Main entrance lobby
30 Detail of entrance lobby fountain
31 View towards the city from the executive conference suite
32 View of internal lightwell

South Bank Arts Centre

Design/Completion 1985/1990
The South Bank, London SE1
The South Bank Board/Stanhope Properties
Approximately 1.5 million square feet master plan area
Existing concrete structures reclad; new buildings in steel and concrete
frame with a variety of external materials

The South Bank has grown since 1951 to become Europe's largest arts and entertainment centre. Essentially, however, it operates as a number of internalised spaces connected by an unsatisfactory system of upper-level walkways, and the outdated buildings do not easily accommodate changing public demands and programming ideas. The master plan takes the Royal Festival Hall and National Theatre as its focal points, and provides new and replacement arts venues organised around a network of pedestrian routes at ground level, with parking and servicing arranged so as to free most of the site for pedestrians. The involvement of different architects, artists, landscape designers and craftsmen will ensure architectural diversity, and the addition of shops, restaurants and office space will add the urban colour and activity which are lacking in the existing single-user complex. Also improved are the waterside and public spaces which are such an asset to the South Bank, both as part of the visitor's experience and in the view from the Thames.

1

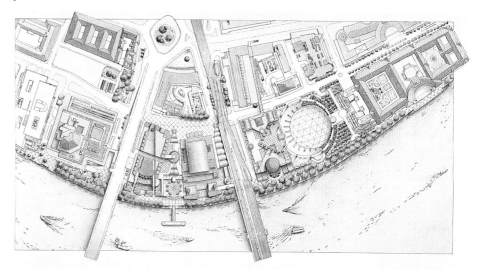

2

3

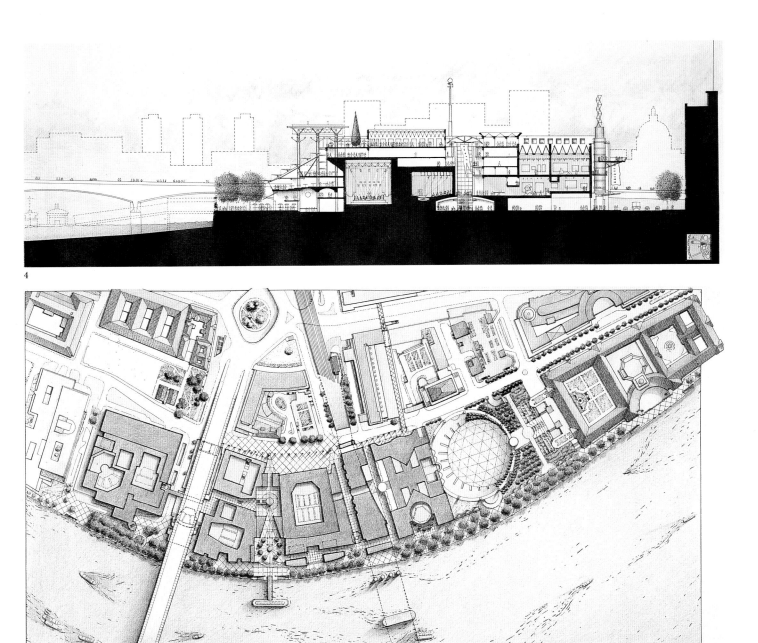

1 Existing view
2 Master plan
3 The South Bank Arts Centre as existing
4 Section through Queen Elizabeth Hall
5 Public spaces: new uses
6 Axonometric

7

8

7 Model: aerial perspective
8 Location plan: South Bank Arts Centre
highlighted
9 Concept sketch
10 Concept sketch: the river frontage
11 Concept sketch: perspective
12 Model: river elevation
13 Model: view from Westminster

9　　　　　　　　　　　　　　　10　　　　　　　　　　　　　　　11

12

13

Alban Gate

Design/Completion 1987/1992
125 London Wall, London EC2
MEPC Developments Ltd
650,000 square feet
Steel frame; arched columns; Macolloy bars
Granite faced stainless steel; prefabricated steel truss
panels; polyester powder coated double-glazed windows;
planar glazing and special metalwork

The redevelopment of Lee House
is a substantial urban design project
forming part of an overall plan for the
redevelopment of existing office buildings
along London Wall in the City of London.
It incorporates a new public square,
housing, shops and restaurants, as well
as forming a gateway to the Barbican
Centre. The office building consists of two
linked blocks over the road intersection
of London Wall and Wood Street: the
Lee House block on the site of the old
structure and the Air Rights block
spanning the road. At podium level,
the project provides retail accommodation
fronting onto pedestrian areas which are
integrated with the existing Barbican
walkways in the immediate vicinity.
A smaller-scale annexe known as the
west wing comprises office, retail and
residential accommodation, and the
existing Monkwell Square is re-landscaped
in a traditional manner. Two basement
levels beneath Lee House, the west wing
and the square accommodate offices,
plant and car parking.

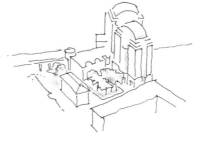

1

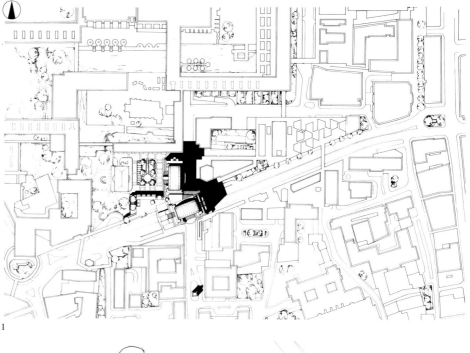

2

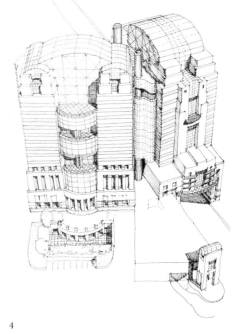

4

3

5

6

7

1   Roof plan in context
2   Conceptual sketch
3   Early conceptual perspective
4   Early conceptual perspective
5   Wood Street elevation
6   Night elevation
7   View from the city, with the Barbican
    Centre behind

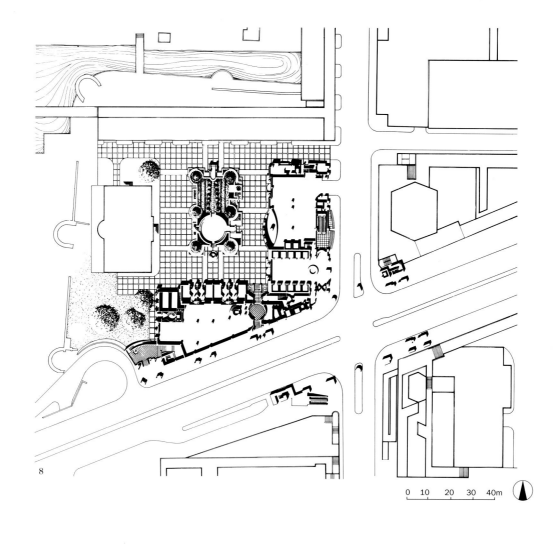

8

0 10 20 30 40m

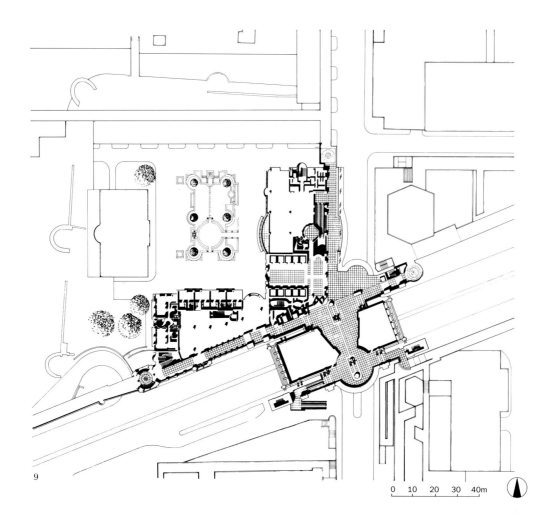

9

0 10 20 30 40m

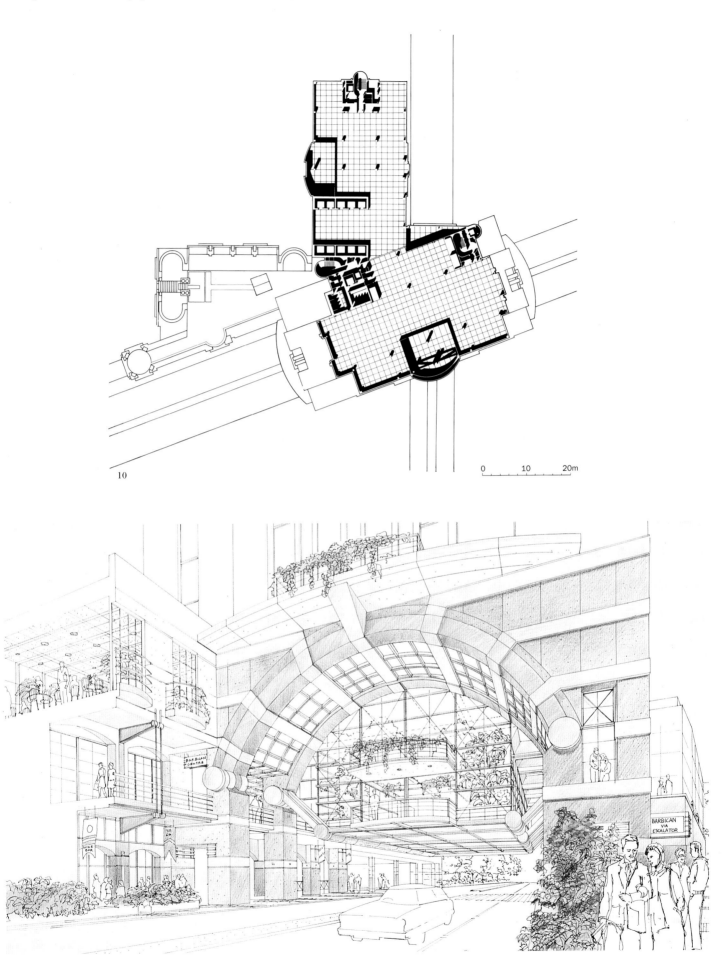

10

0   10   20m

11

12

13

14

15

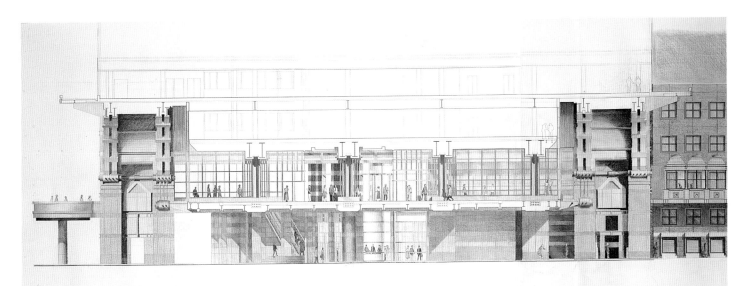

16

12 Monkwell Square
13 Detail of escape stairs and rooftops
14 Aerial perspective from the north-west
15 External elevation of atria at night
16 Part section through pedestrian walkway
17 Night elevation: detail

17

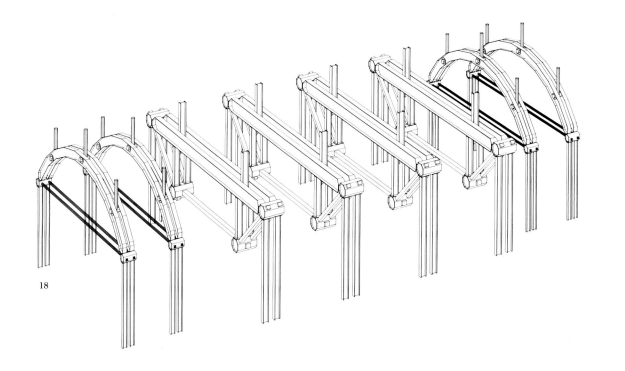

18

19

20

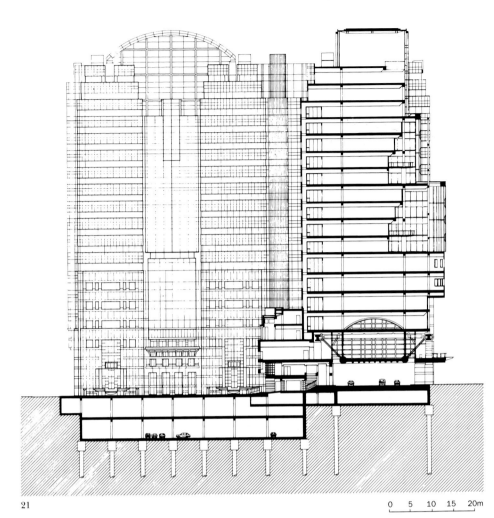

18 Transfer structure
19 West wing, north elevation
20 West wing, south elevation
21 Cross section through Air Rights building
    (north–south)
22 Detail of arch beneath the Air Rights building
    and the west wing
23 Monkwell Square

21

0 5 10 15 20m

22

23

24

25

26

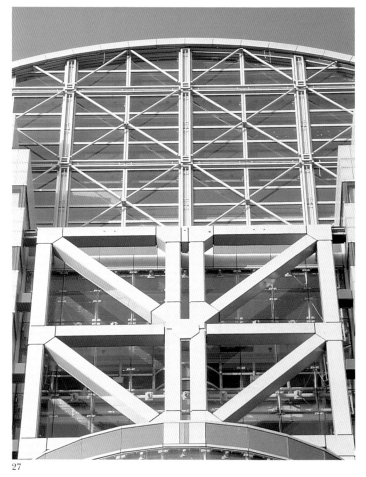

27

28

Moor House

Design/Completion 1991
London Wall, London EC2
Greycoat PLC
398,000 square feet
Steel frame
Granite cladding panel; fritted glazed panel; coloured glass spandrel;
glazed curtain wall; polyester coated and anodised metal louvres;
metal panel mullions and transoms

The Moor House proposal, like Alban
Gate, involves the replacement of a 1960s
office block with a new building that
responds to the requirements and patterns
of the surrounding context, and relates to
the urban characteristics of boundary and
gateway. A new public concourse was
established at ground level, which forms
the principal entrance to the building
and connects the Crossrail and Moorgate
transport interchanges to the Barbican
Centre. A new bridge links the concourse
with St Alphage High Walk, across London
Wall to the Guildhall and the City. Inside
Moor House new public spaces provide a
variety of civic amenities beneath the vast
atrium located in the centre of the
building. The building is treated as a
series of connected mini-blocks, with
a 2-storey elevation on Moorgate, and
a 20-storey facade adjacent to London
Wall. The elevation articulates the
tripartite division found in good street
architecture.

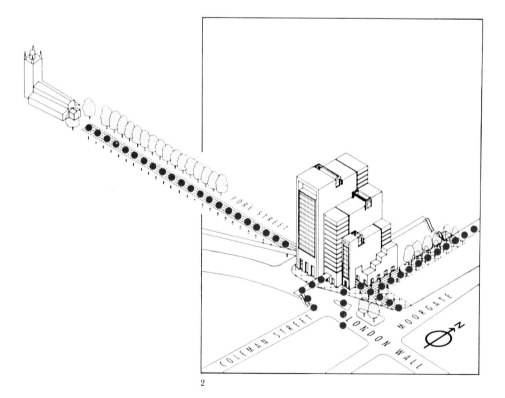

1

2

128

1 Aerial photograph of London Wall and the Barbican Centre, with the existing Moor House highlighted
2 Aerial perspective in relation to St Giles, Cripplegate
3 Model photograph
4 East elevation across London Wall
5 Public circulation: ground level
6 Public circulation: podium level

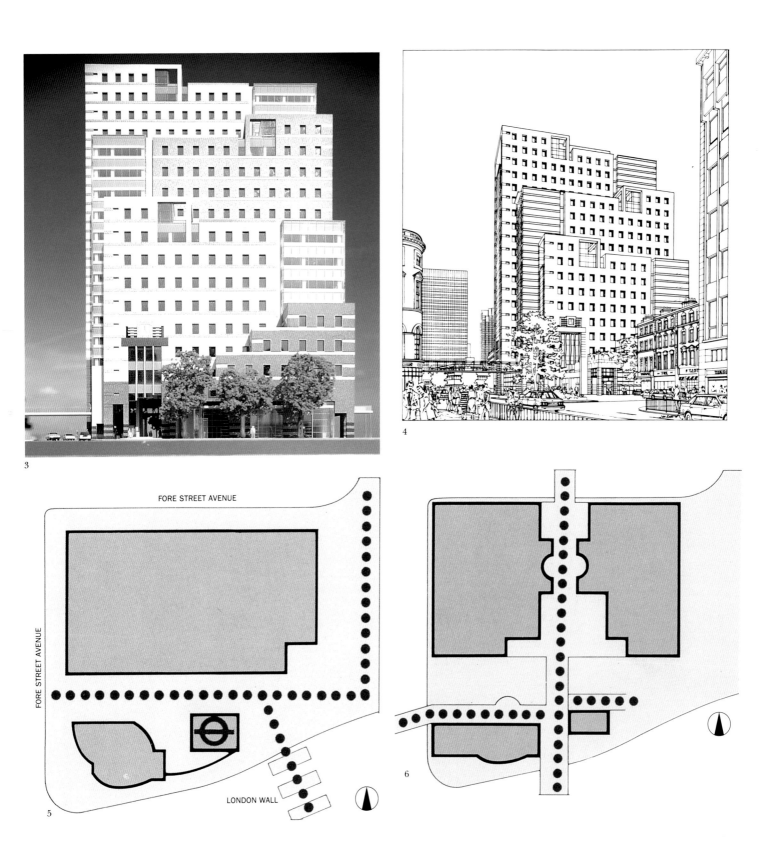

3

4

FORE STREET AVENUE

FORE STREET AVENUE

LONDON WALL

5

6

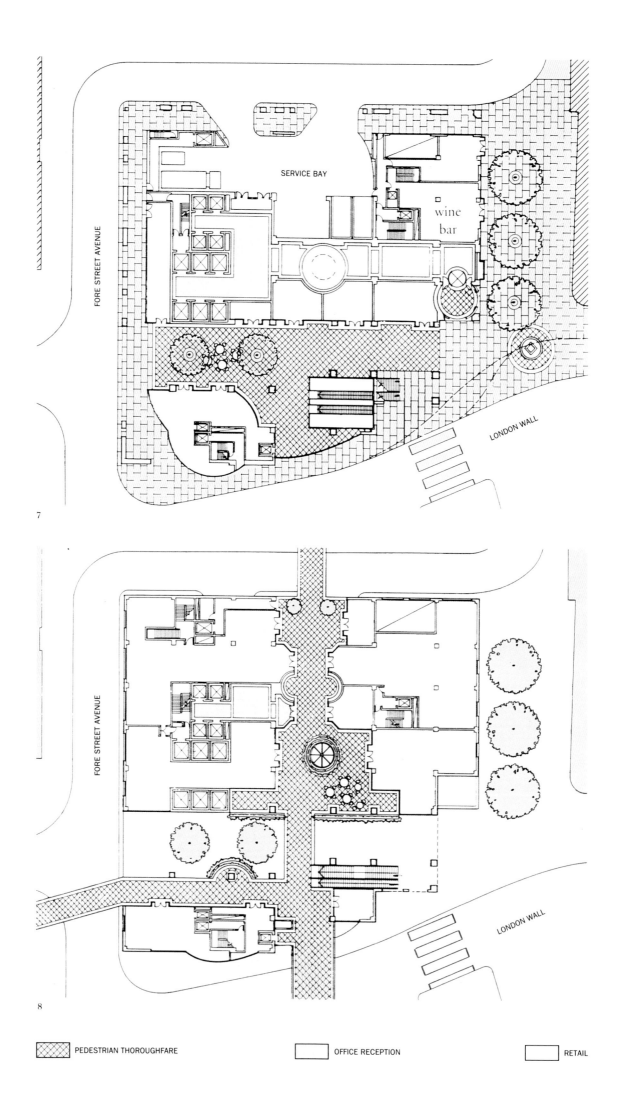

FORE STREET AVENUE

SERVICE BAY

wine bar

LONDON WALL

7

FORE STREET AVENUE

LONDON WALL

8

PEDESTRIAN THOROUGHFARE

OFFICE RECEPTION

RETAIL

7 Ground-floor plan
8 Podium-level plan
9 East elevation from Moorfields
10 South elevation from London Wall
11 Part east elevation
12 Part south elevation

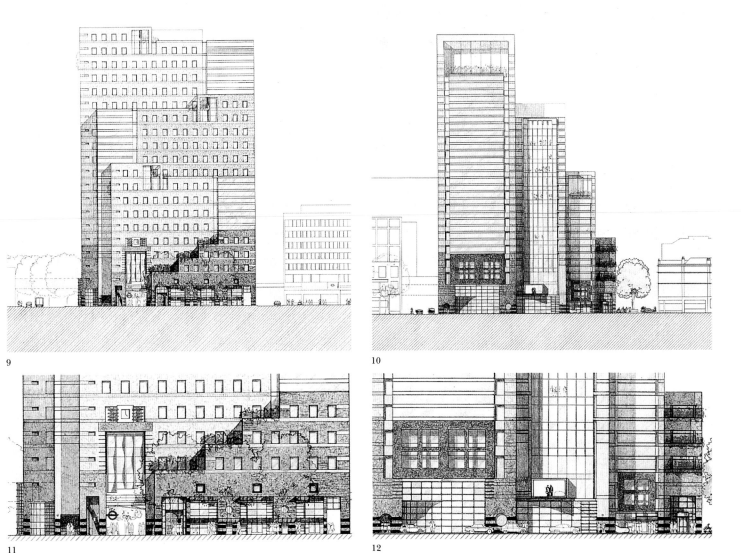

9

10

11

12

13 Location plan
14 Perspective view north across London Wall
15 Model photograph

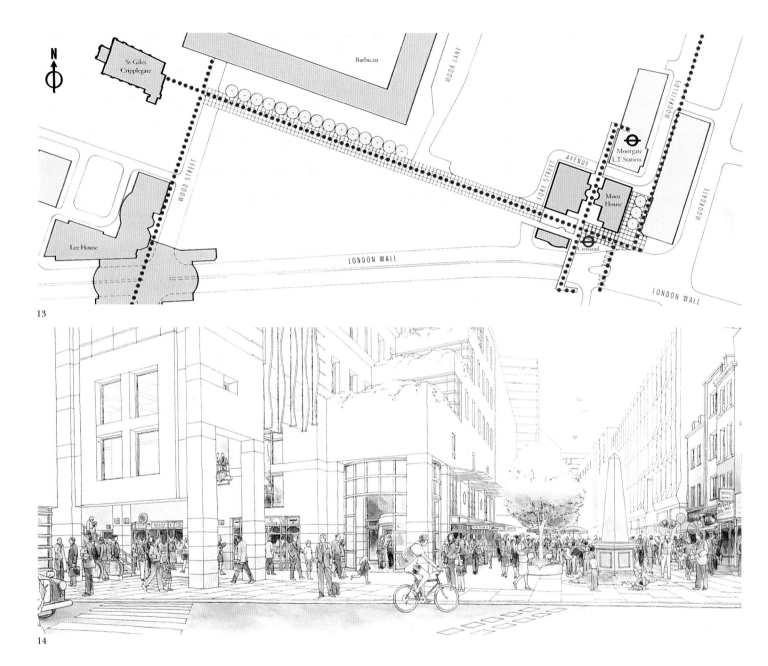

13

14

Government Headquarters Building (MI6), Vauxhall Cross

Design/Completion 1988/1993
Albert Embankment, London SE1
The British Government Property Services
in conjunction with Regalian Properties
420,000 square feet
In situ reinforced concrete frame and floor slabs
Metal/glass curtain walling and precast concrete
cladding

This bespoke office headquarters building for a government department, on the banks of the River Thames, includes the construction of a new landscaped river wall, esplanade and gardens.

The building is a group of three longitudinal blocks—low-rise on the river side and medium-rise onto Albert Embankment—which are linked by glazed courtyards and atria. The building is set back from the river on a perpendicular axis. The Albert Embankment elevation incorporates the main frontage and entrance to the building. This provides the most suitable massing and micro-climatic arrangement, and also allows views of the river from within the site, the riverside walkway and the land to the east of the site.

The public will have access to the riverside along the newly formed, landscaped riverside walkway from both Vauxhall Cross and the Albert Embankment.

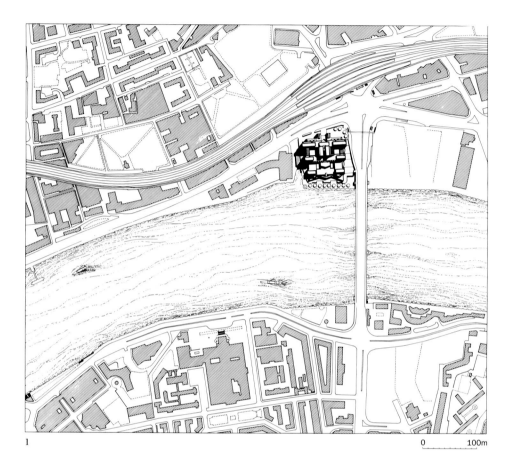

1   0   100m

2

1   Roof plan in context
2   North elevation
3   River elevation
4   Detail of north elevation
5   Detail of north elevation from level three terrace

3

4

5

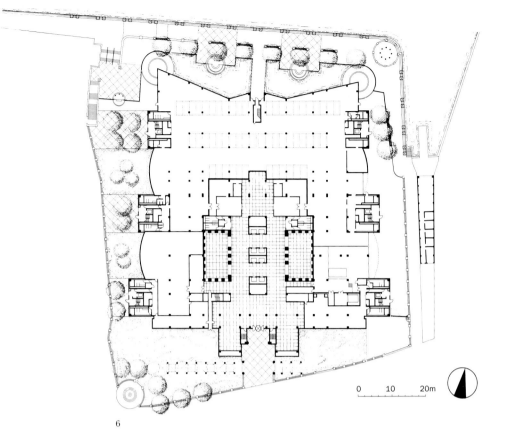

6

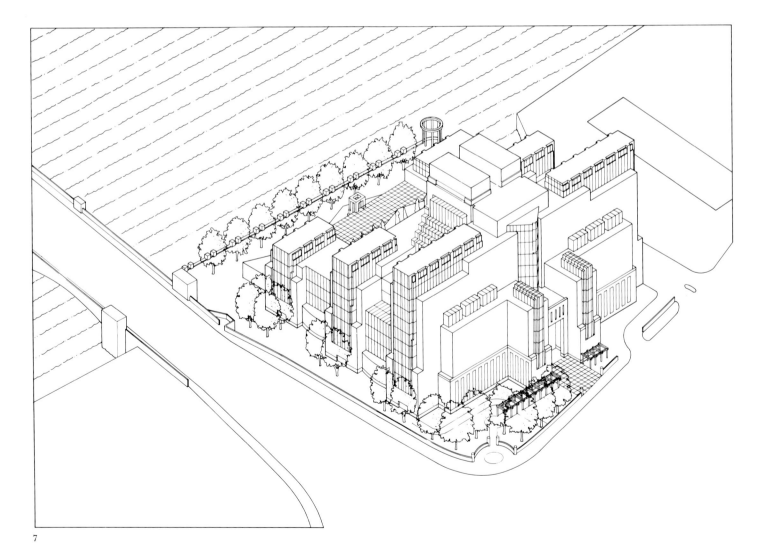

7

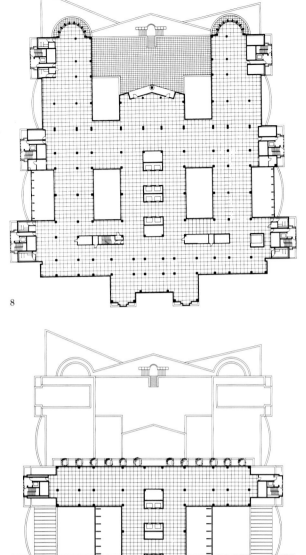

8

9

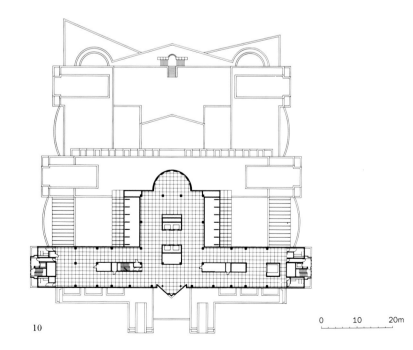

10

0   10   20m

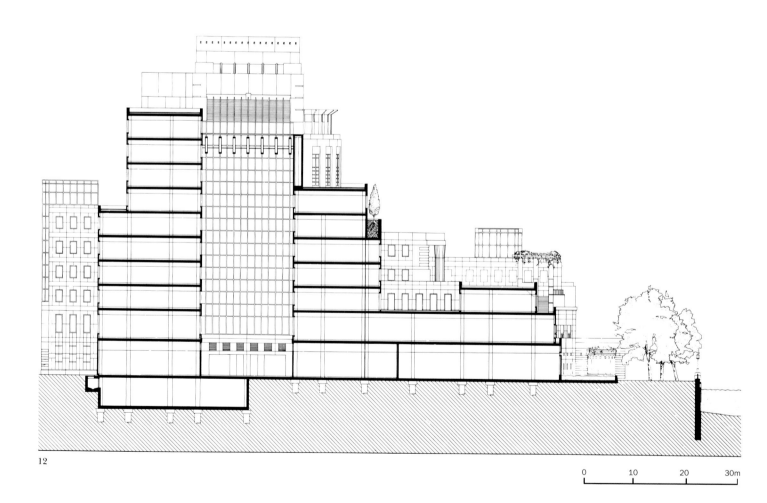

11

12

0   10   20   30m

13

14

15

16

17

18

19

17 Detail of south elevation
18 Detail of main entrance, south elevation
19 West elevation
20 Detail of main entrance, south elevation

20

21 Entrance towers as seen through the pergola
22 Main entrance gates
23 Detail of main entrance, south elevation

21

22

Chiswick Park Master Plan

Design/Completion 1989
London W4
Stanhope Trafalgar Chiswick
Site area: 32 acres
Master plan infrastructure design: defining spaces, squares and patterns
of circulation, which provides the framework for future development
Landscaping completed 1992

This site is located midway between Central London and Heathrow, adjacent to a nature reserve. It was formerly a bus works for London Transport and had no obvious identity from which to develop a "mid-urban" business park. The scheme raised sensitive issues, and demanded much consultation with an articulate and politically aware local community.

Terry Farrell was appointed as master planner and architect, coordinating building designs by leading British architects including Foster Associates, Richard Rogers Partnership, Ahrends Burton & Koralek, Peter Foggo Associates and Eric Parry Associates. The master plan establishes a central square and avenue along with landscape and infrastructure framework designed and detailed in collaboration with Hannah/Olin Ltd and Ove Arup Partners. It provides for improved public transport, with a new privately funded bus route through the site, and indoor and outdoor recreation amenities for employees. Building plots allow for maximum design flexibility and future expansion.

1

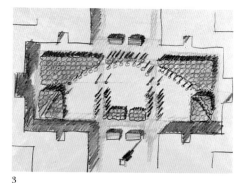

2

3

4

1 Master plan model
2 Central square landscaping
3 Central open space landscaping study
4 Arrival square landscaping study
5 Concept drawing: landscaping, early option
6 Axonometric of building D, in context
7 Part view into atria, building D model
8 Master plan, 1989
9 Central square landscaping: view towards building D
10 Central square landscaping: view towards building D

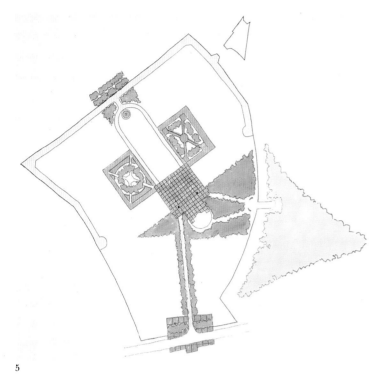

5

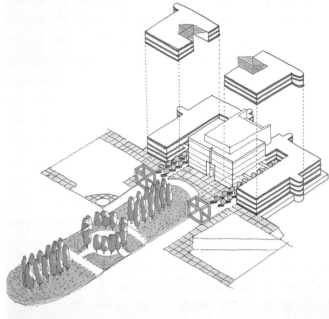

6

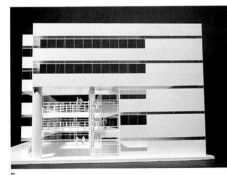

7

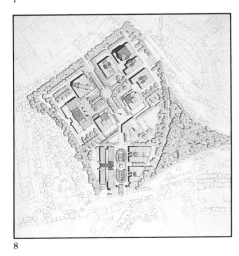

8

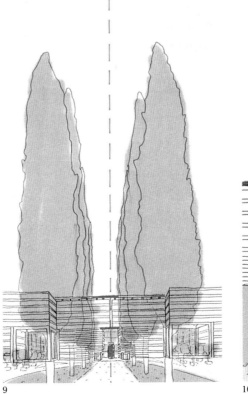

9

10

ABK Bldg @ angle to view →

what is this plant?
Zelkova? Ash?

11

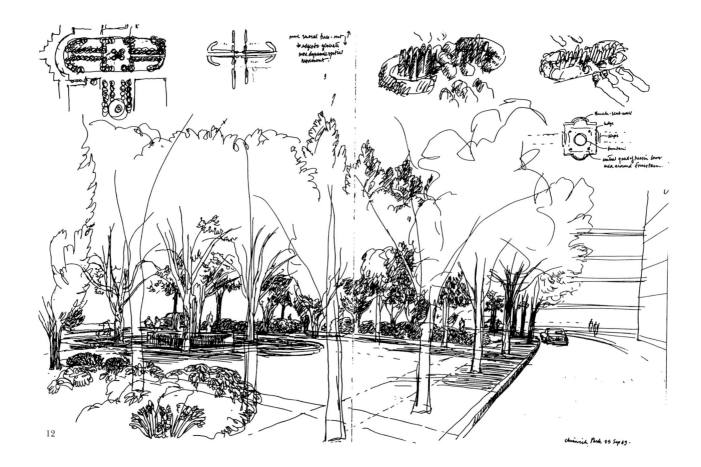

none sacral trees - not ?
to adjust to geometry
more dynamic spatial
movement

Bench - seat - wall
ledge
steps
fountain
central quad of trees in lawn
area around fountain.

12

Chiswick Park 25 Sep 89.

11 Landscaping sketch
12 Landscaping sketch
13 Landscaping concept drawing
14 Landscaping: Orchard Avenue
15 Concept drawing: atria relating to landscape
16 Concept drawing: front doors relating to landscape

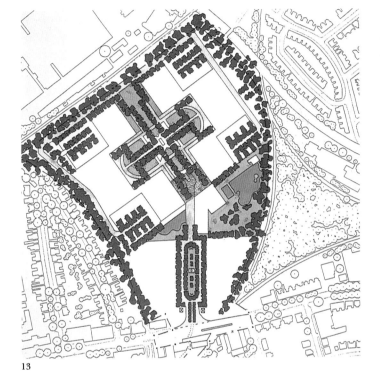

13

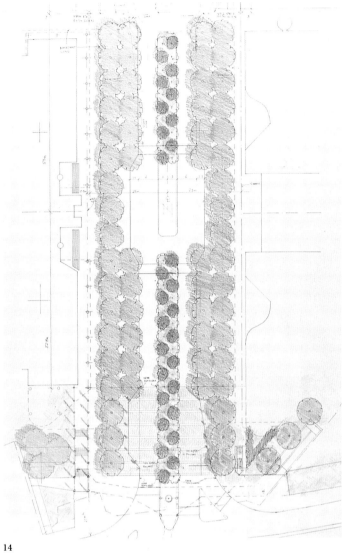

14

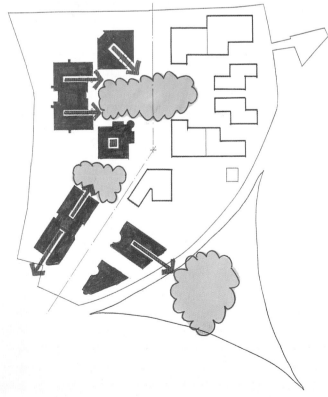

15

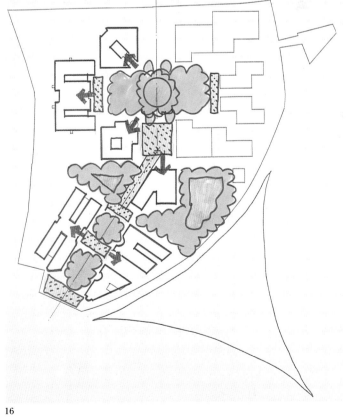

16

Lloyds Bank Headquarters, Pall Mall

Design/Completion 1991
Waterloo Place, London WC2
Lloyds Commercial Property Investments Ltd
108,000 square feet
Proposed refurbishment and conversion of an existing building
Existing steel framed stone clad building extensively
adapted/rebuilt in matching materials

Further automation of the banking process and decentralisation of work will drastically reduce the number of staff employed at the Waterloo Place branch of Lloyds Bank. This situation has led Lloyds to examine options for the future use of their building.

The current street layout, including the facades onto the street, was designed by Nash, although the site has been rebuilt many times since then. Terry Farrell's proposals conserve as much of the existing building fabric as possible. The elevations are retained, and new servicing and roof-top plant designed in sympathy, while inside high-specification office accommodation is provided within a flexible internal layout allowing for either a cellular or an open-plan arrangement. The east elevation and internal structure will be replaced with a flat-slab concrete structure to allow for primary distribution of services. Floor levels are maintained as existing, allowing retention of staircases at either end of the building.

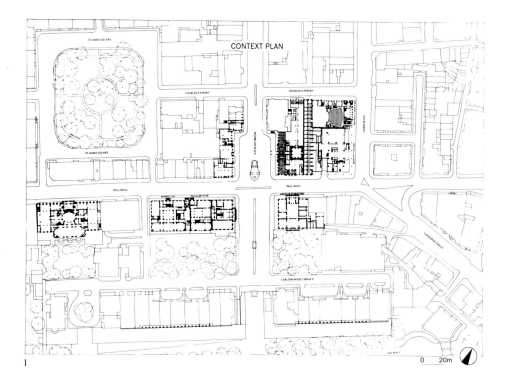

1

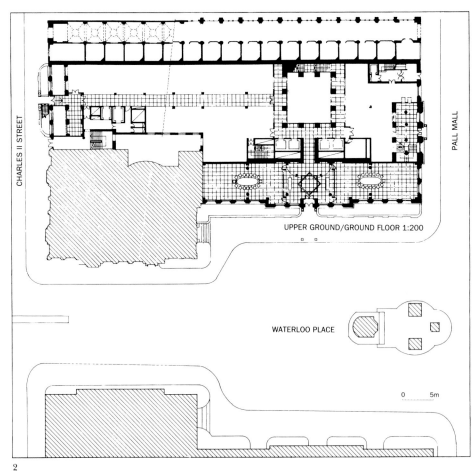

2

1 Context plan
2 Floor plan
3 Waterloo Place
4 Existing bank interior
5 The Grand Room: internal elevations and plans
6 Concept study: cross section
7 The Grand Room: perspective

8

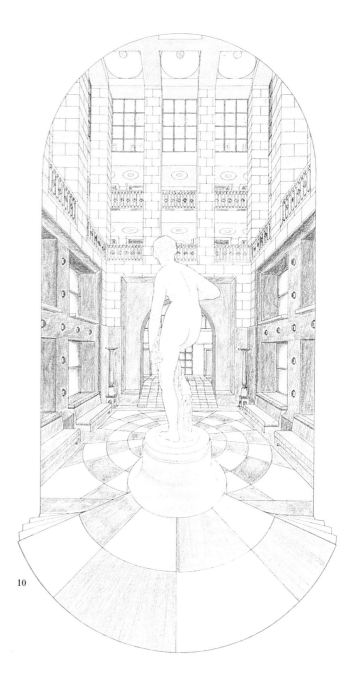

10

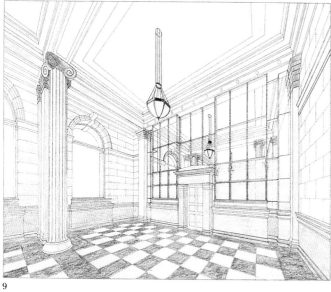

9

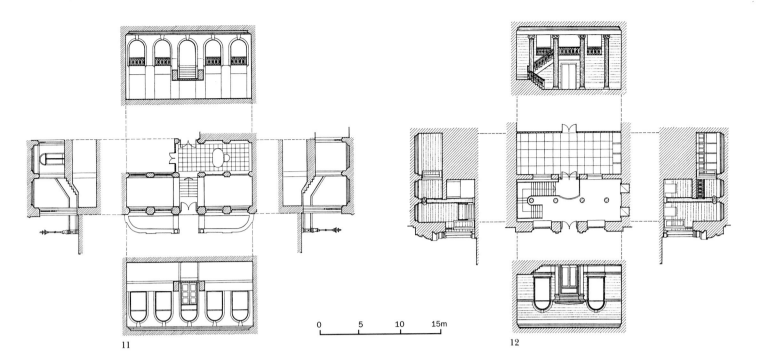

11

12

0   5   10   15m

13

Commonwealth Trust Offices and Club

Design/Completion 1991
18 Northumberland Avenue, London WC1
Commonwealth Trust
105,000 square feet
Proposed refurbishment and conversion of an existing building
Existing steel framed stone clad building, extensively adapted/rebuilt
in matching materials

The present proposal for the building
arose out of a recent reappraisal, by the
Commonwealth Trust and their financial
and property advisers, of the changing
needs of the Trust. Many of the rooms
in this large building are under-used,
and the building fabric is also in need
of remedial work.

The purpose-built headquarters of 1868
were of a modest club appearance,
reflecting the French Renaissance fashion
of the period, and flanked by Craven
House and the Turkish Baths. The Society
flourished and expanded so that after the
Great War two designs were presented
by the architects Hart and Waterhouse
for a much larger Royal Empire Society
in Northumberland Avenue. The Society
eventually proceeded with Sir Herbert
Baker RA, FRIBA instead: an apposite
choice, since Baker was, through his
prolific work in Africa and India, the
pre-eminent architect of the Empire.

1

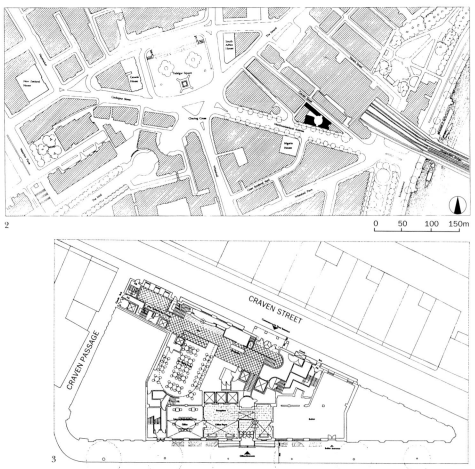

2

0   50   100   150m

3

NORTHUMBERLAND AVENUE

1   Model: view of corner elevation from the River Thames
2   Location plan
3   Ground-floor plan
4   Model: aerial view from the north
5   Aerial perspective of Northumberland Avenue
    elevation viewed from the River Thames
6   Proposed Commonwealth Trust elevation, Craven Street

4

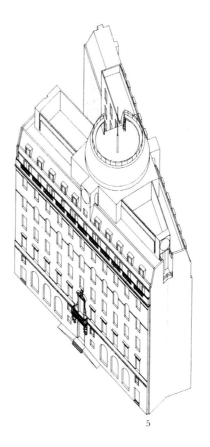

5

6

Brindleyplace Master Plan

Design/Completion 1990
Birmingham
Shearwater Property Holdings PLC
19.2-acre master plan
130,000 square feet (shopping and restaurant); 1 million square feet (office accommodation); 200,000 square feet (leisure); 2,600 car parking spaces

Brindleyplace lies immediately next to Birmingham's National Indoor Arena and International Conference Centre. It is central to the city's strategic plan to expand the centre westwards and raise the city's national and international profile.

This development accommodates extensive new office and shopping space, entertainment and leisure facilities and a major hotel, and restores important local landmarks.

The master plan reinforces the new civic axis between the city centre and the convention centre, projecting it to the centre of the site and terminating in a new city square. This square acts as a focus for routes linking the various parts of the site with one another and with the major civic amenities already provided around the perimeter.

1

2

3

4

1 Detail of the master plan
2 Canalside building study
3 Canalside building studies
4 Model: aerial view
5 Rational building plots
6 Aerial perspective: massing study
7 Aerial perspective: massing study
8 Sequence of urban spaces
9 "Central spine": open spaces
10 Canalside walkway

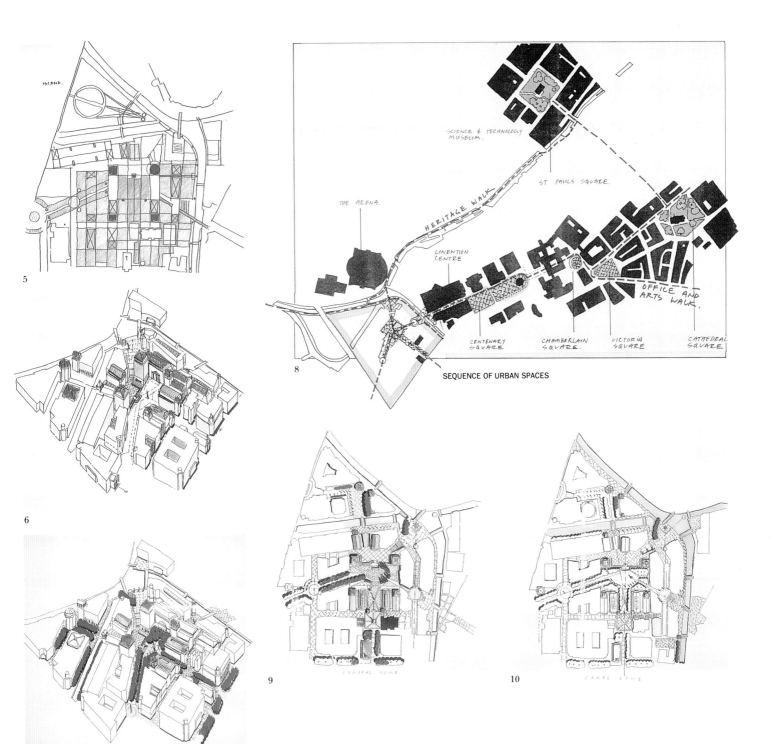

SEQUENCE OF URBAN SPACES

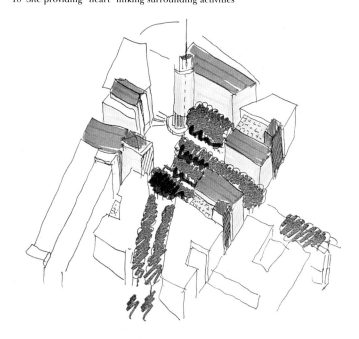

landscape

11

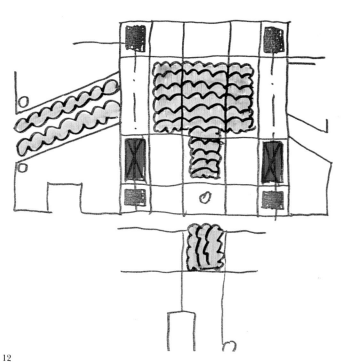

12

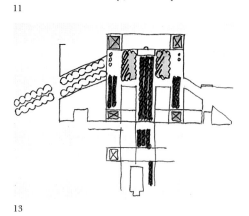

13

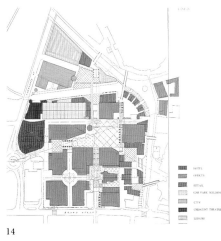

14

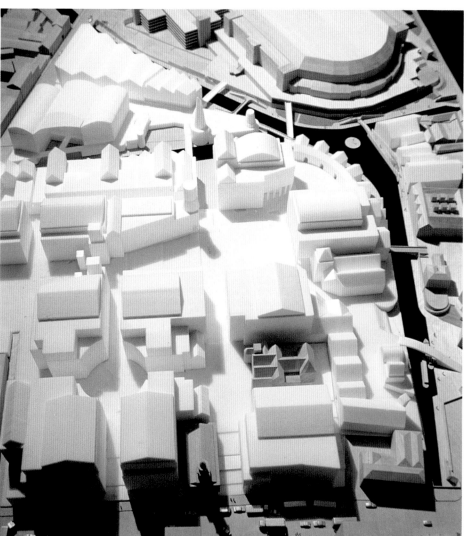

15

16

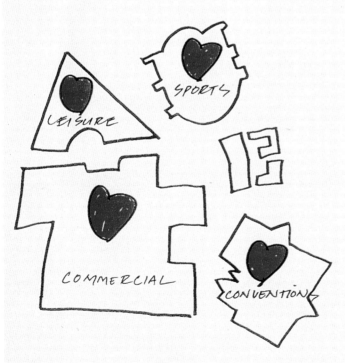

17

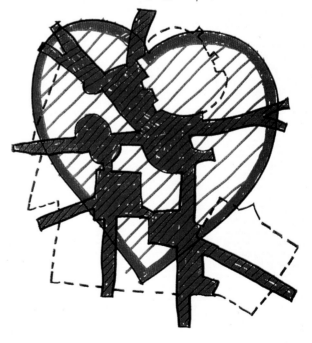

18

Thameslink 2000, Blackfriars Bridge Station

Design/Completion 1991/1993
London EC4
British Railways Board
885,100 square feet
Curved glazed canopy on steel frame; set upon an existing historic
Victorian bridge

Thameslink 2000 forms a crucial part
of the ambitious scheme to improve the
whole rail network throughout the country
and enable trains from Europe to travel
directly to the north of England without
stopping at a London terminus.

The commission involves presentation
of evidence for the parliamentary bill,
preparation of master plans for the major
stations along the route, proposals for
development where the opportunity
arises in several important central
London locations, and for urban design,
planning and architectural responses
to the environmental impact of British
Rail's engineering works.

Work at Blackfriars consists of the
provision of a new through-station across
the River Thames, with platform access
from both river banks. Consideration
is given to the environmental implications
of the work, in consultation with those
whose properties or interests are affected
by the proposals.

1

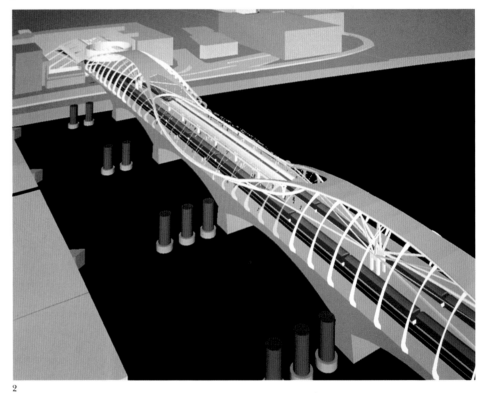

2

1 Night perspective photomontage
2 Computer generated aerial perspective
3 Model: aerial view facing south
4 Canopy study: existing and proposed
5 3-D sketch diagram of existing Blackfriars North
6 3-D sketch diagram of proposed Blackfriars North
7 Axonometric of canopy detail

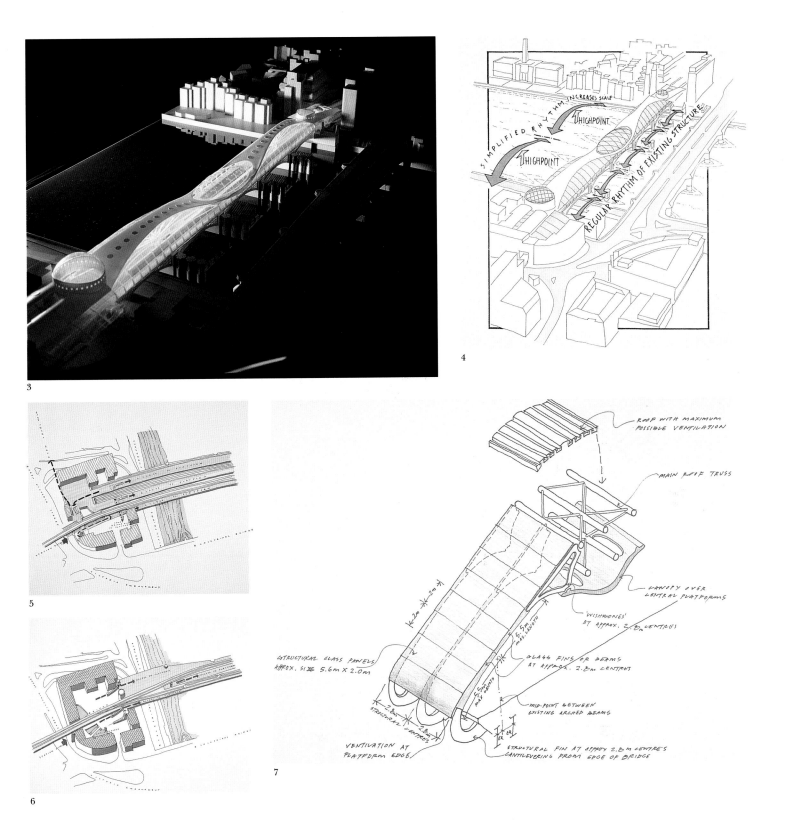

3

4

5

6

7

ROOF WITH MAXIMUM POSSIBLE VENTILATION

MAIN ROOF TRUSS

CANOPY OVER CENTRAL PLATFORMS

'WISHBONES' AT APPROX. 2.8m CENTRES

GLASS FINS OR BEAMS AT APPROX. 2.8m CENTRES

MID-POINT BETWEEN EXISTING ARCHED BEAMS

STRUCTURAL GLASS PANELS APPROX. SIZE 5.6m X 2.0m

VENTILATION AT PLATFORM EDGE

STRUCTURAL FIN AT APPROX 2.8m CENTRES CANTILEVERING FROM EDGE OF BRIDGE

SIMPLIFIED RHYTHM INCREASES SCALE

HIGHPOINT

HIGHPOINT

REGULAR RHYTHM OF EXISTING STRUCTURE

8

9

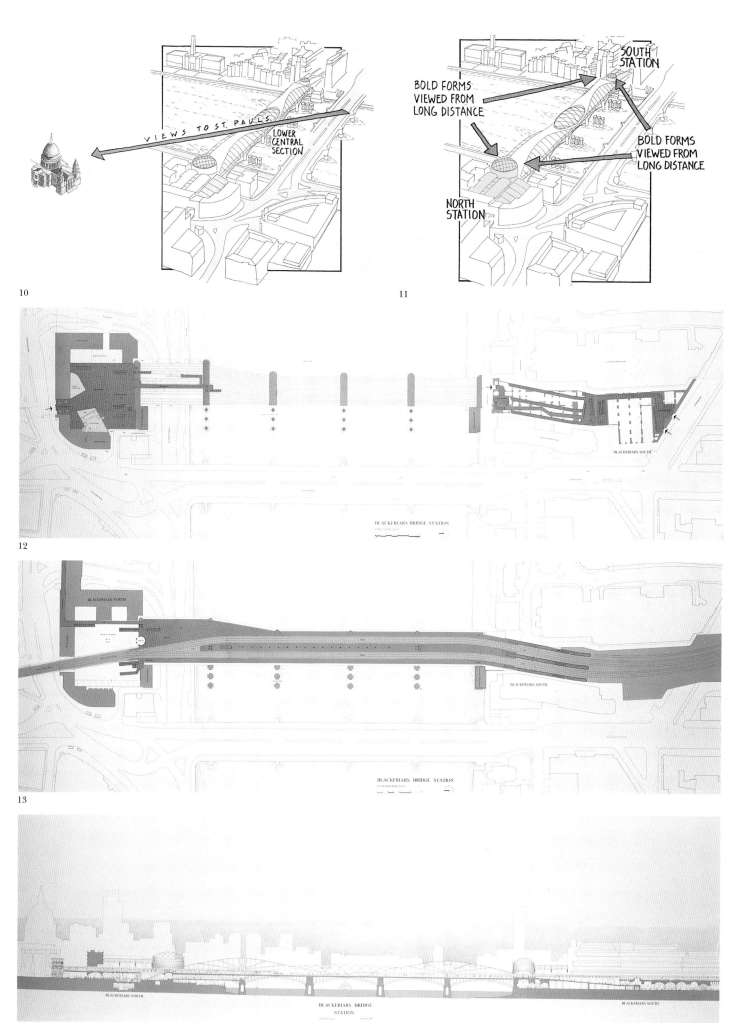

10

11

SOUTH STATION

BOLD FORMS VIEWED FROM LONG DISTANCE

BOLD FORMS VIEWED FROM LONG DISTANCE

VIEWS TO ST. PAULS

LOWER CENTRAL SECTION

NORTH STATION

12

BLACKFRIARS SOUTH

BLACKFRIARS BRIDGE STATION

13

BLACKFRIARS NORTH

BLACKFRIARS SOUTH

BLACKFRIARS BRIDGE STATION

14

BLACKFRIARS NORTH

BLACKFRIARS BRIDGE STATION

BLACKFRIARS SOUTH

15 Canopy option study model
16 Canopy option study model
17 Model: aerial view
18 Model: aerial view facing south-west
19 Model: river elevation
20 Model: aerial view facing south-east

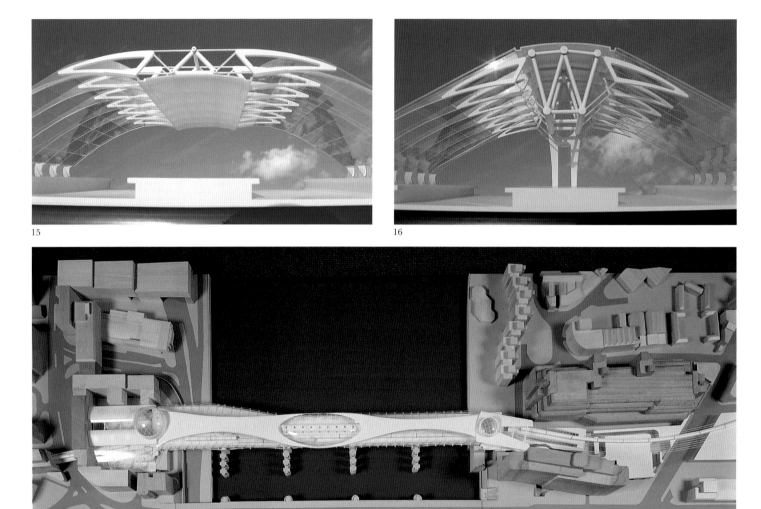

15

16

17

18

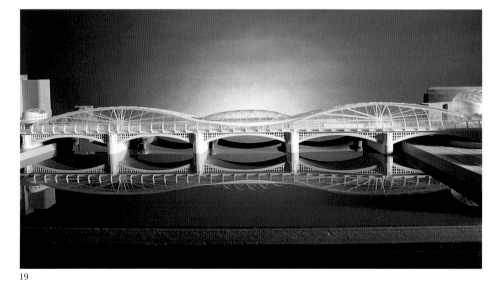

19

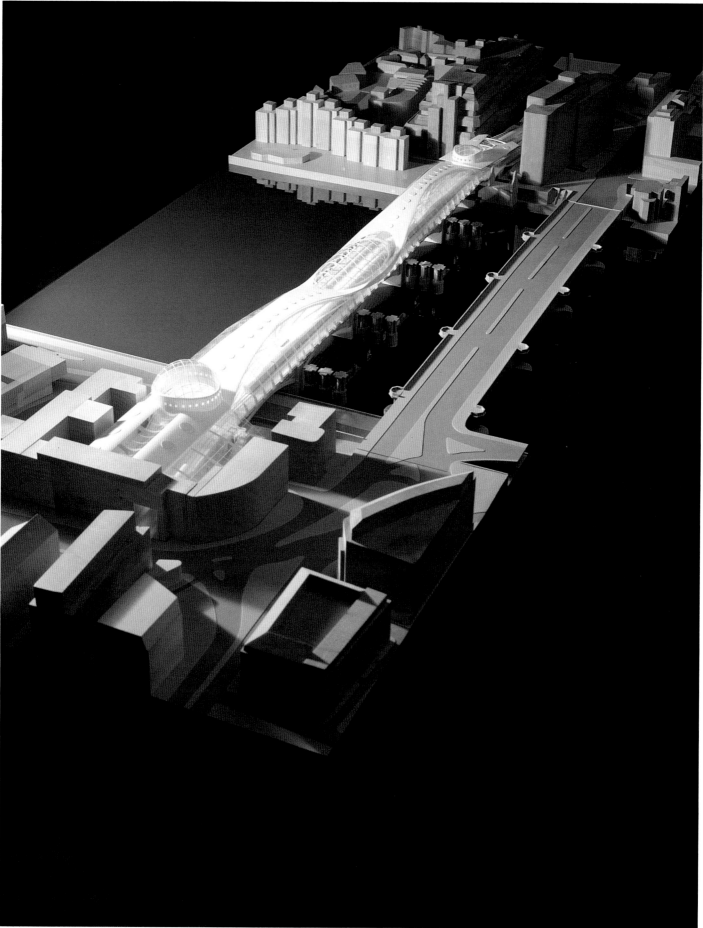

Paternoster Square Master Plan

Design/Completion 1989/planning application 1993
London EC4
Paternoster Associates (Greycoat PLC, Park Tower Group and an affiliate of Mitsubishi Estate Co. Ltd)
1,215,856 square feet
Reinforced flat concrete slabs
Traditional materials
Walls: natural stone, brickwork; architecturally precast stone
Roof: slate; copper and lead

The aim of the proposals is to revitalise the area immediately to the north of the most important building in the City of London, St Paul's Cathedral, improving the quality of the environment for those who visit and work in the area. A balanced mix of buildings, public spaces, gardens, shops, wine bars and restaurants is set within the reinstated traditional pattern of streets and lanes. The architecture respects the traditions of the City, using materials such as stone, brick, tile, slate and copper, and views of St Paul's are restored from Paternoster Square at ground level, and on the skyline. Re-establishment of pedestrian routes into the site creates a new, traffic-free, public open space.

Terry Farrell is working as coordinating master planner with two other master planners, Thomas Beeby and John Simpson, and has collaborated with five other architects in the design of the individual buildings. Planning permission was granted in 1993. This scheme has received the 1994 AIA Urban Design Award in the USA.

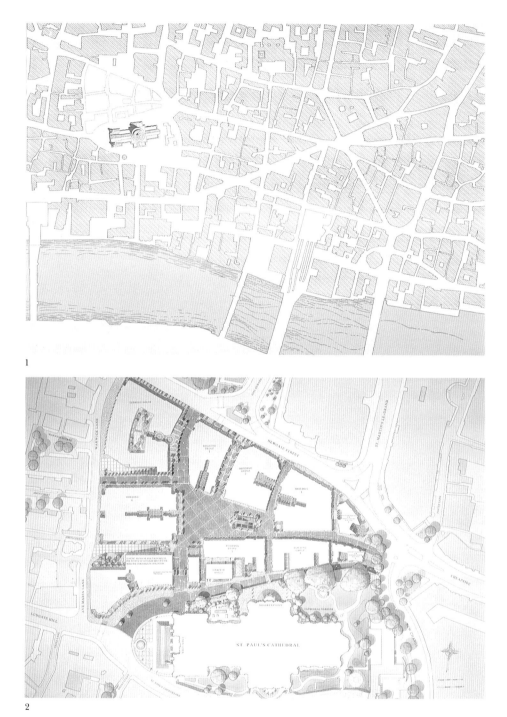

1

2

1 The master plan restores the urban grain of the surrounding area
2 The master plan, 1992
3 Perspective view into Paternoster Square, looking east
4 The master plan in the city context
5 Holford's Plan, 1956
6 The master plan

3

4

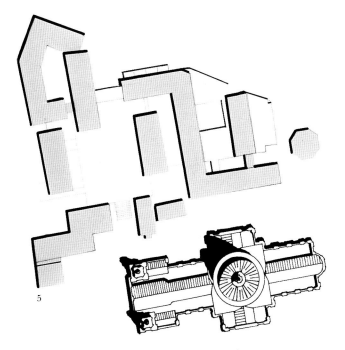

5

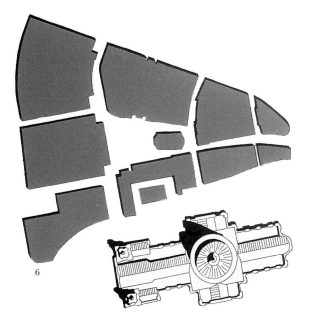

6

7 Existing development based on a rigid grid at right angles to the cathedral
8 The master plan restores the traditional pattern of curving streets and lanes
9 The traditional alignment of St Paul's churchyard
10 The existing St Paul's churchyard
11 The master plan restores St Paul's churchyard
12 Paternoster Square building elevation, building group 1

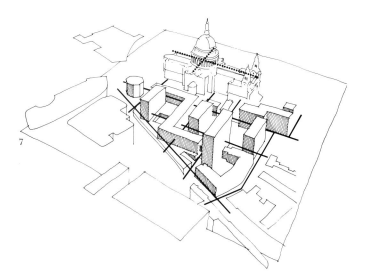

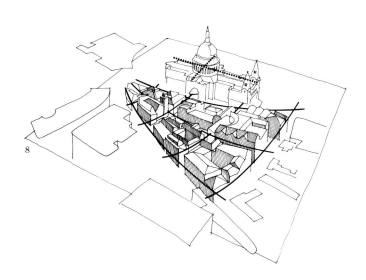

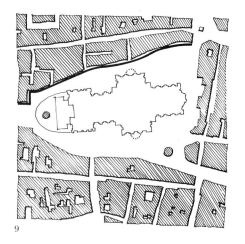

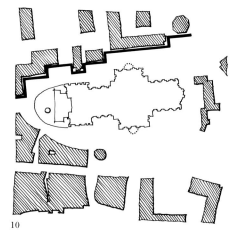

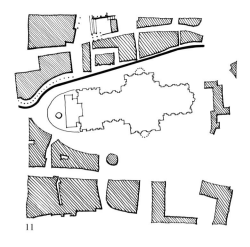

12

13 View south down Ivy Lane Arcade
14 Newgate Street looking east towards Cheapside
15 Ivy Lane Arcade
16 Newgate Street building elevation, building group 2

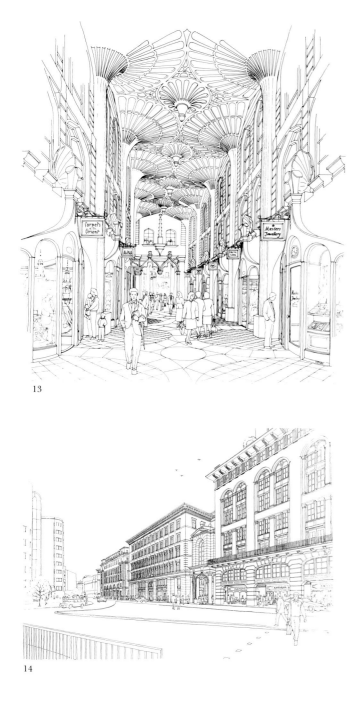

13

14

IVY LANE ARCADE
Between Building Group 1 & 2

15

NEWGATE STREET BUILDING

Building Group 2

Terry Farrell & Company

MCMXC

Edinburgh International Conference and Exhibition Centre

Design/Completion 1989/1995
Morrison Street, Edinburgh, Scotland
Edinburgh District Council, Lothian & Edinburgh Enterprise Limited and
Lothian Regional Council
133,000 square feet
In situ concrete frame up to ground floor and all core levels; steel frame
to drum from ground floor up
Sandstone; architectural precast concrete; metal rails; profiled metal panels
and louvres; structural double-glazing; glass blocks; membrane roof

The development of the winning master plan proposals by Terry Farrell during 1989 and 1990 led to the location of the Conference Centre at the crossing of Morrison Street and the West Approach Road: a prominent position at the centre of the emerging West End/Port Hamilton/Haymarket business district, on the western approach to the city.

The Conference and Exhibition Centre design has been influenced by the shape of the site, the difference in levels between Morrison Street and the West Approach Road, budget restrictions, and its role in the realisation of the master plan.
It establishes the setback and curve of the Morrison Street frontage and pedestrian access from Morrison Street.
A simple, strong architecture is intended to give the building both civic presence appropriate to its Scottish setting, and an international image. In keeping with the master plan principles, the elevations will be light buff/grey in colour, harmonising with the traditional sandstone of Edinburgh.

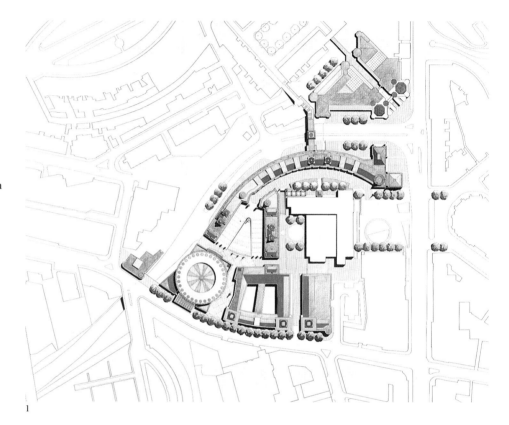

1

2

3

1 Master plan, 1993
2 Perspective view
3 West elevation
4 Level 2 plan, lower-ground level

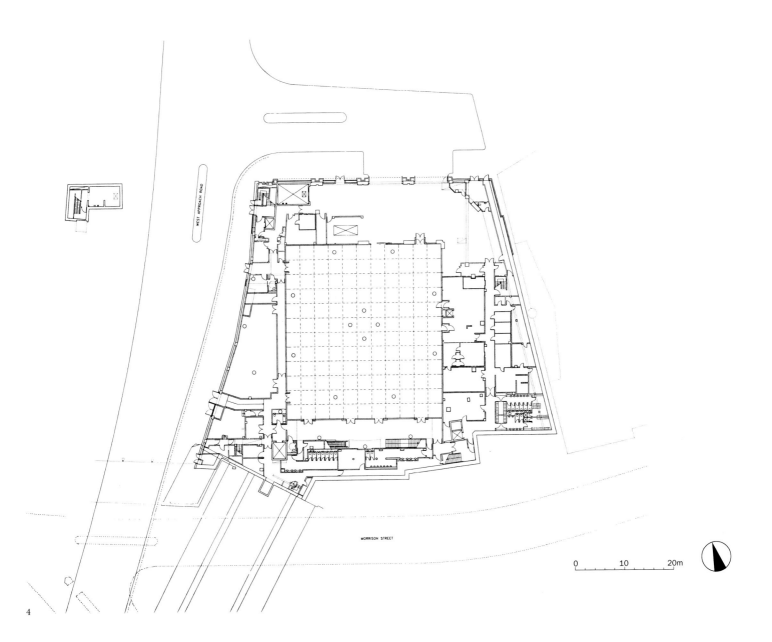

4

5

6

172

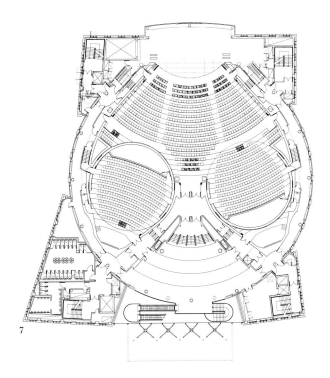

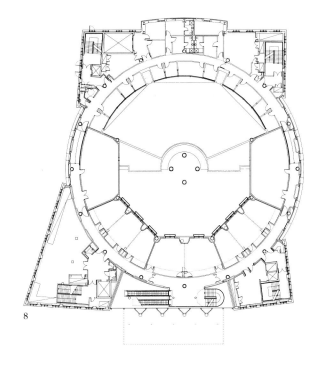

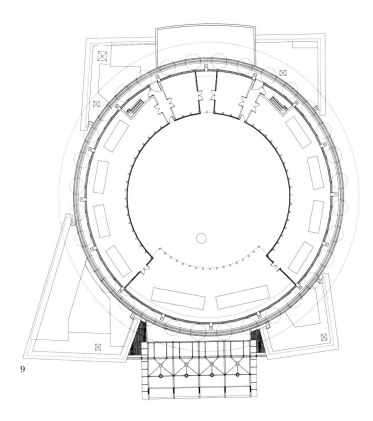

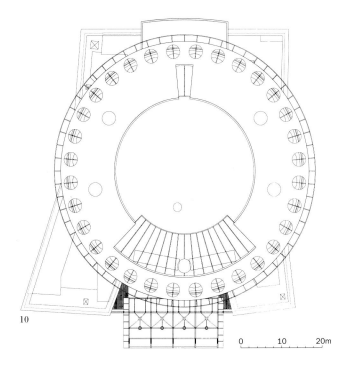

7

8

9

10

0   10   20m

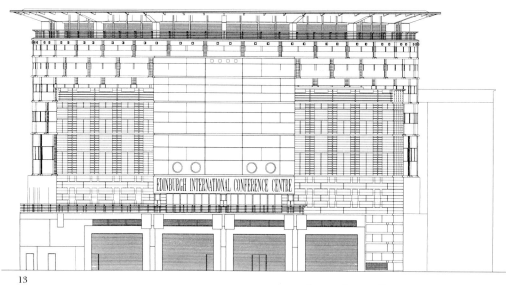

11

12

13

EDINBURGH INTERNATIONAL CONFERENCE CENTRE

0   5   10   15m

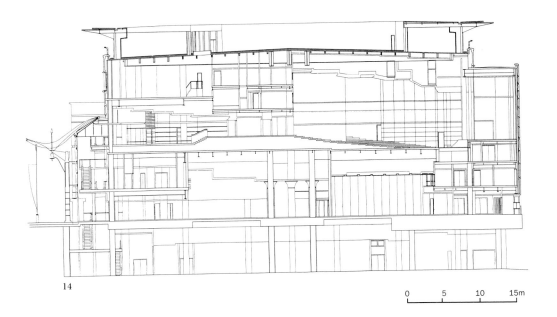

14

0   5   10   15m

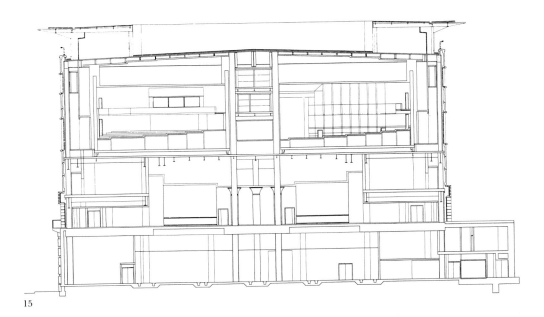

15

16 Model: aerial view
17 Model: west elevation
18 Model: detail of south elevation, main entrance
19 Construction shot: view looking west from Morrison Street
20 Model: canopy detail

16

17

18

19

20

Westminster Hospital Redevelopment, Horseferry Road

Design/completion 1991/1994
St John's Gardens, Horseferry Road, London SW1
Westminster Hospital in conjunction with British Land PLC
Master plan: 684,940 square feet
Concrete frame
Brick; stone; metal and glass cladding

North West Thames Regional Health Authority, working with British Land PLC, commissioned Terry Farrell to create a mixed-use scheme for the replacement of the complex of buildings comprising Westminster Hospital. Investigation of mixed-use solutions involving redevelopment and/or conversion of this prominent site in a commercial environment is under way. This involves full negotiation with adjoining owners, planning authorities, highway authorities and other agencies, and coordination of the full range of building and landscape services to achieve the objectives. The scheme includes 131 flats/maisonettes, 417,750 square feet of offices, a day-care centre for the elderly, a nursery school/creche, shops, restaurants and the redesign and revitalisation of the garden square amenities. Detailed planning permission was granted in February 1994.

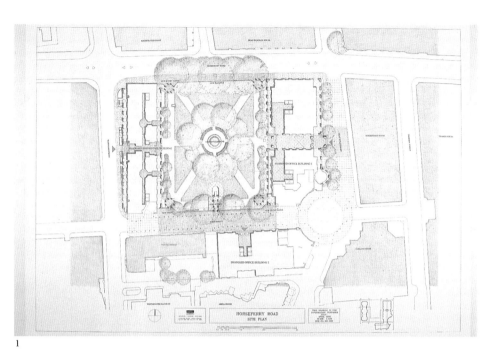

1

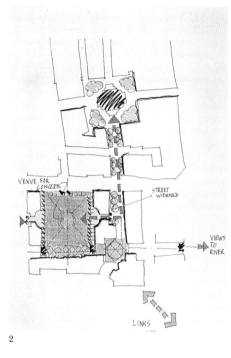

2

3

1   Master plan, June 1992
2   Conceptual sketch
3   Model: aerial facing north-east
4   Typical upper-floor plan showing range
    of residential apartments
5   Typical floor plan showing the efficient and
    flexible office space
6   Marsham Street elevation from St John's Gardens
7   Dean Ryle Street elevation and link to Page Street

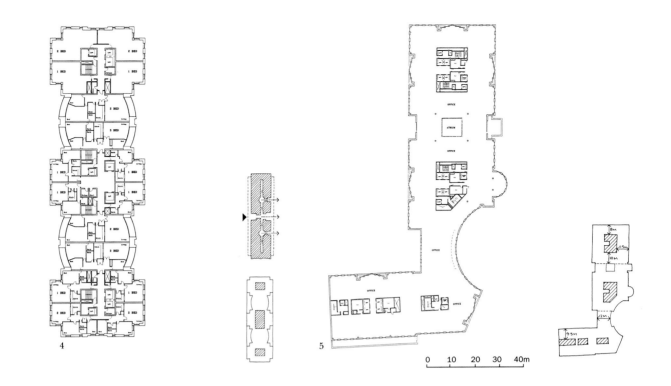

4

5

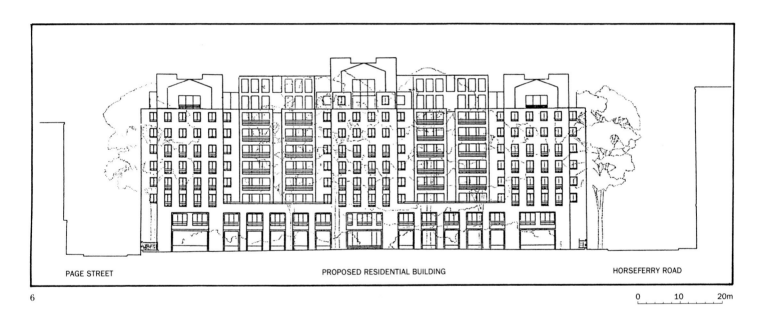

0   10   20   30   40m

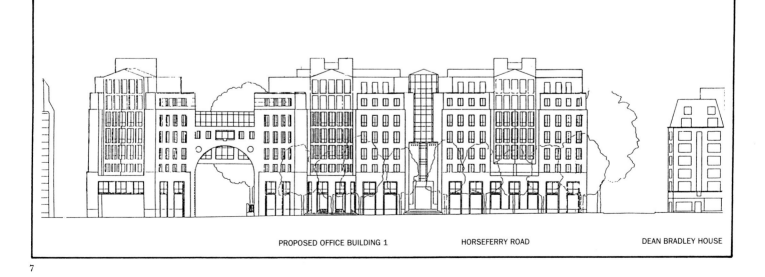

PAGE STREET   PROPOSED RESIDENTIAL BUILDING   HORSEFERRY ROAD

6

0   10   20m

PROPOSED OFFICE BUILDING 1   HORSEFERRY ROAD   DEAN BRADLEY HOUSE

7

The Peak Tower, Hong Kong

Design/Completion 1991/1995
Hong Kong
The Hong Kong and Shanghai Hotels Ltd
118,000 square feet
Reinforced concrete
Natural anodised aluminium cladding; metal and glass cladding;
suspended double glazed walls; architectural ceramic tiles

This was the winning entry in a limited international competition for a landmark building to replace the existing Peak Tower on a prominent site in Hong Kong. It commands one of the best views in the world and creates a backdrop to the spectacular cityscape of Hong Kong's central district.

The building is highly visible and is intended to symbolise Hong Kong. The form is open to many symbolic interpretations, including bowl, boat, open hands. The solid base, open podium and floating roof with upswept eaves also refer to traditional Chinese architecture.

The design incorporates the existing Peak tram station, with additional retail and restaurant areas, and a 'special theme ride' located in the podium, ending at the lowest level. Visitors will proceed upwards by escalator or lift to the tram station and main entrance at mid-level, and the viewing platforms and restaurants at the top, passing retail outlets on their way. The project will be completed in 1995.

1

2

1 Aerial photomontage
2 North-west perspective, in context
3 Perspective view from the north-west
4 Perspective view from the north-east
5 Cross section through the Peak Tower

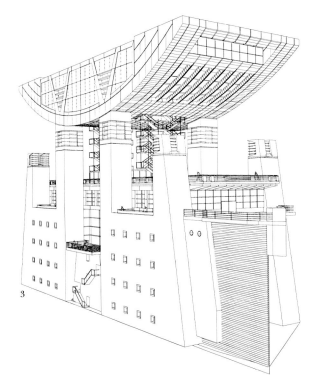

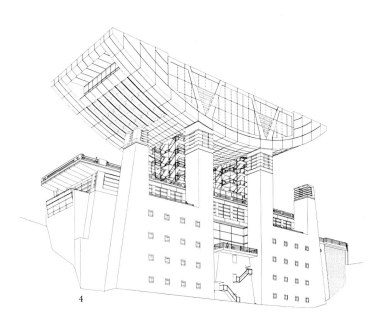

3

4

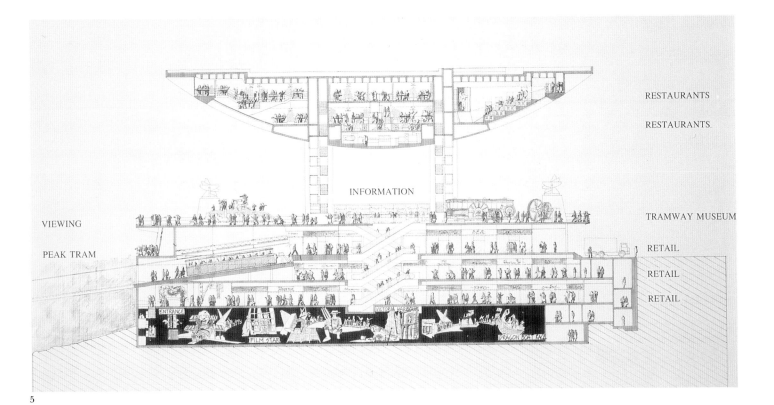

RESTAURANTS

RESTAURANTS

INFORMATION

TRAMWAY MUSEUM

VIEWING

PEAK TRAM

RETAIL

RETAIL

RETAIL

5

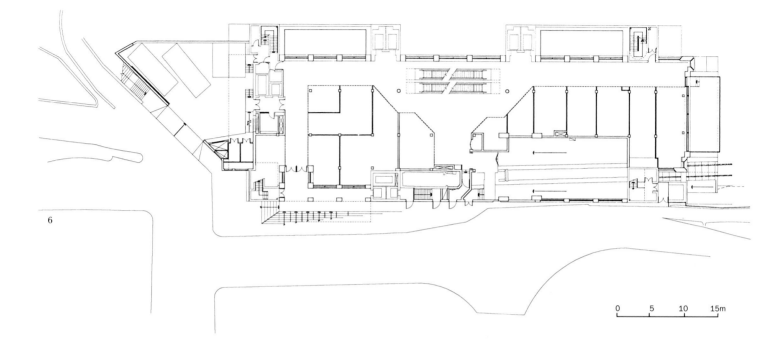

6

0   5   10   15m

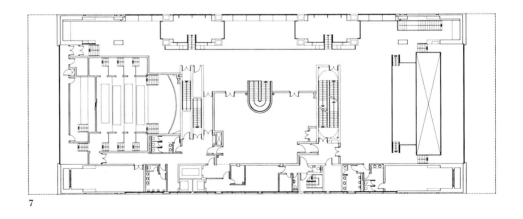

7

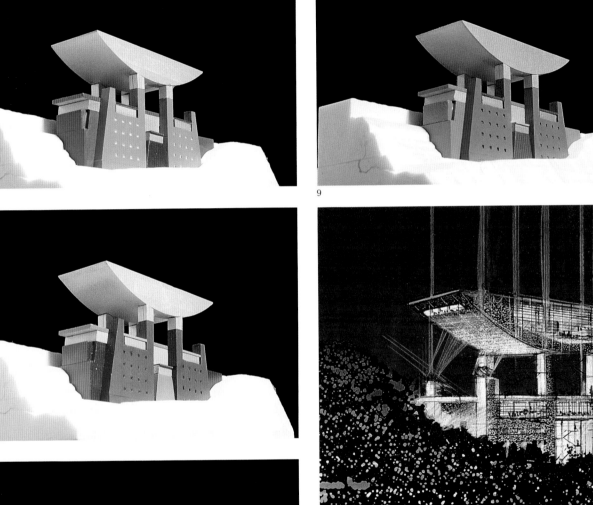

8

9

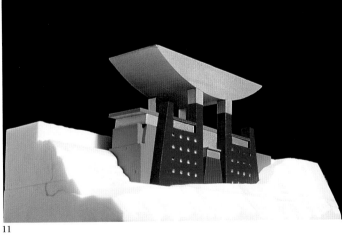

10

11

12

13 Cross section (north-south)
14 East elevation
15 South elevation
16 North elevation

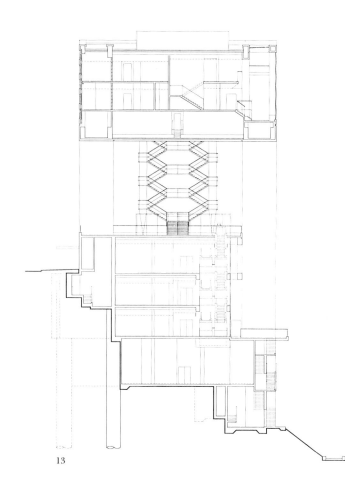

13

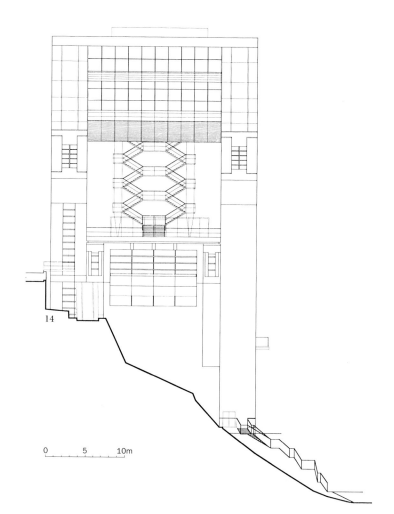

14

0   5   10m

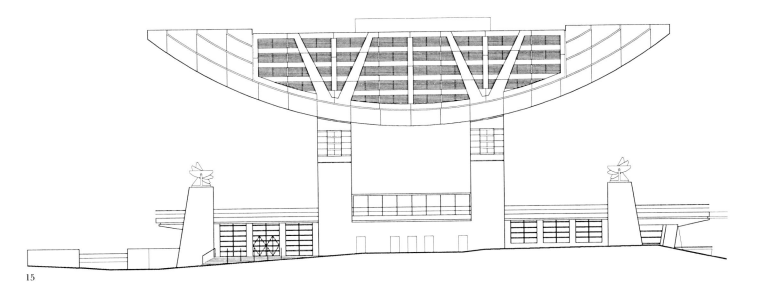

15

0   5   10   15m

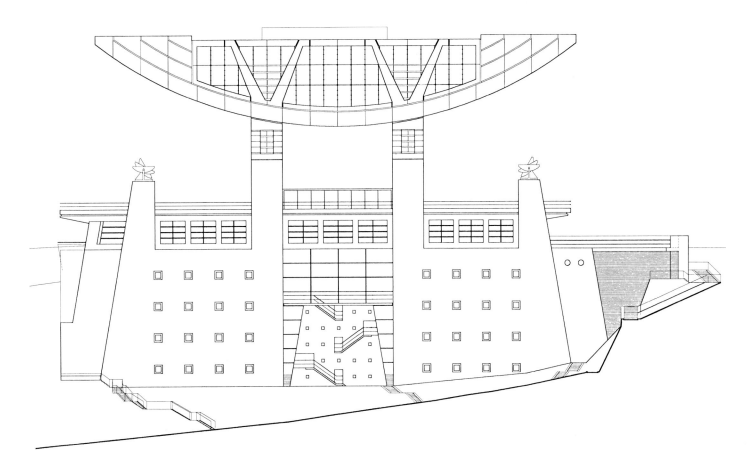

16

17 Perspective view from the north-east
18 Model: north-east perspective
19 Model: north elevation
20 Longitudinal section (east-west)

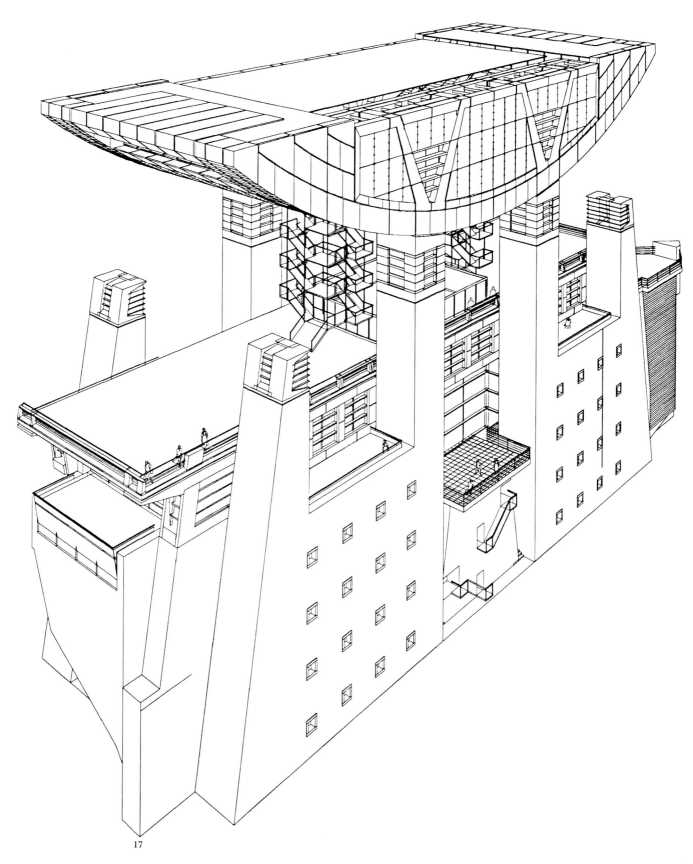

17

18

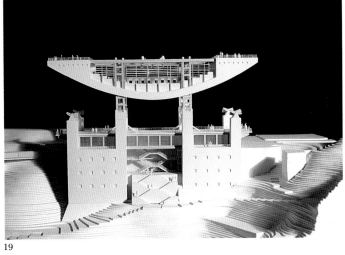

19

20

0   5   10   15m

Headquarters for the British Consulate-General and the British Council, Hong Kong

Design/Completion 1992/1996
Supreme Court Road, Hong Kong
Her Britannic Majesty's Secretary of State for Foreign and Commonwealth Affairs
185,000 square feet
Reinforced concrete
Granite cladding; natural anodised aluminium cladding; render, metal and glass cladding

This important government commission, received as a result of an architectural competition, required a particularly sensitive design approach in view of Hong Kong's prominence on the world stage and the significance of the building, which represents Great Britain's continued interest when Hong Kong becomes a special administration region of China in 1997.

The new headquarters will provide accommodation for both the British Consulate and the British Council on a site adjacent to the new Hong Kong Park. Two perimeter buildings are linked by a common entrance pavilion. The two main buildings have their own position and identity with contemplative views onto the private, secluded gardens, and a long public frontage.

The consistent 10-storey roof-line echoes Hong Kong public buildings of the past. Local climatic conditions prompted the use of passive solar control through brise-soleils and other devices.

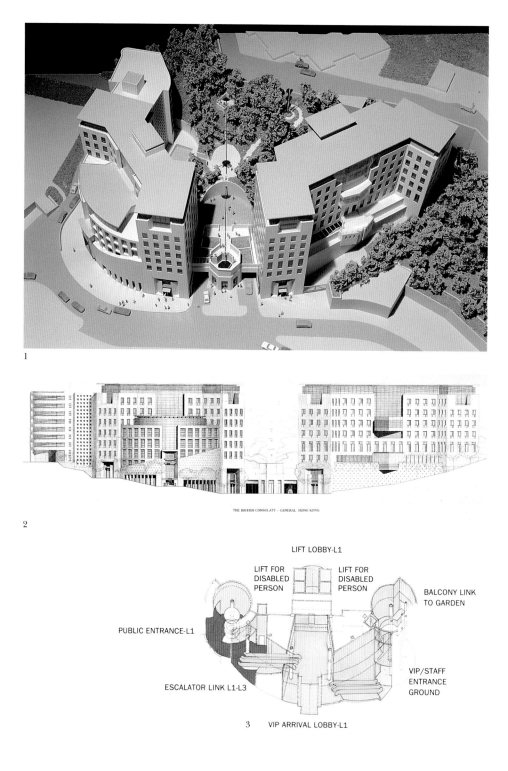

1

2

THE BRITISH CONSULATE – GENERAL HONG KONG

LIFT LOBBY-L1

LIFT FOR DISABLED PERSON

LIFT FOR DISABLED PERSON

BALCONY LINK TO GARDEN

PUBLIC ENTRANCE-L1

VIP/STAFF ENTRANCE GROUND

ESCALATOR LINK L1-L3

3   VIP ARRIVAL LOBBY-L1

1 Model: aerial view
2 East through to west elevation
3 The British Consulate-General: axonometric
4 Figure ground plan: the British Consulate-General Headquarters (left),
  and the British Council Headquarters (right)
5 The British Council: level 1–2 axonometric
6 The British Council: ground-level axonometric

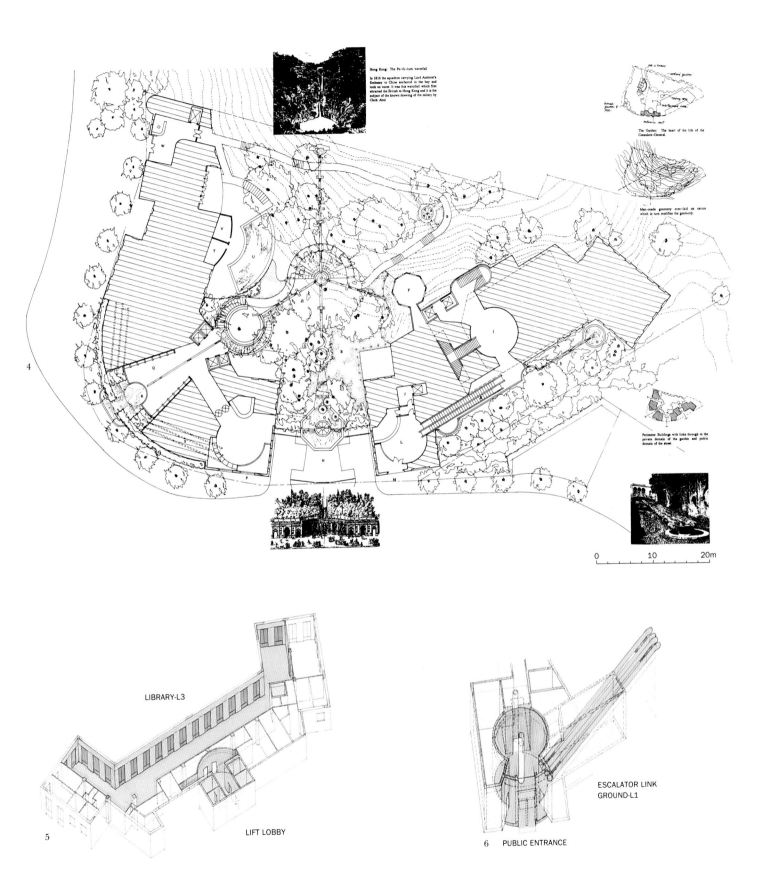

LIBRARY-L3

LIFT LOBBY

ESCALATOR LINK
GROUND-L1

5

6   PUBLIC ENTRANCE

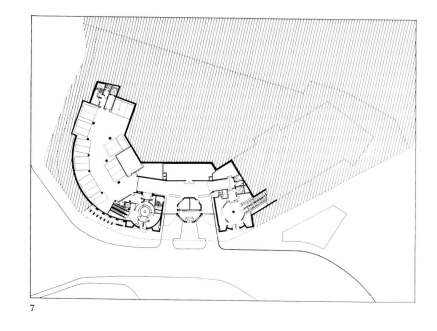

7

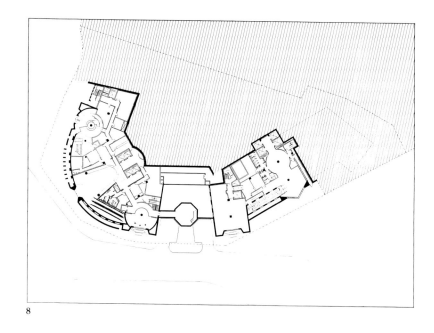

8

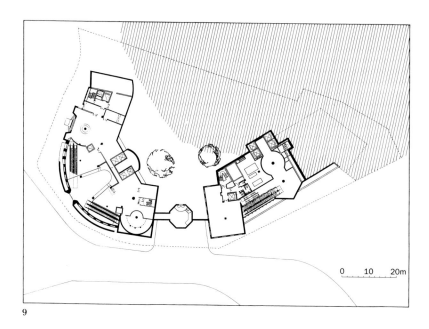

0   10   20m

9

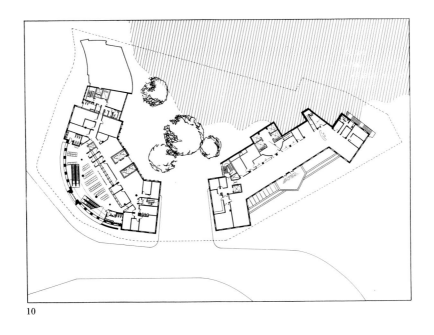

10

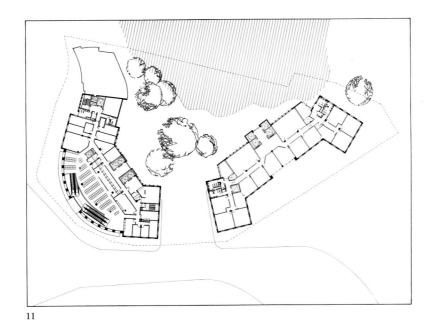

11

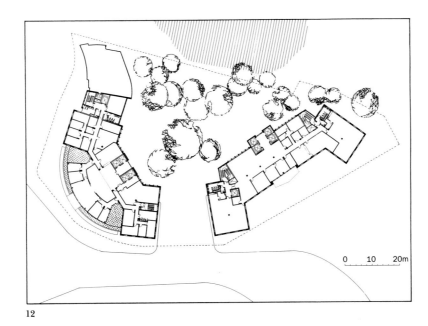

0   10   20m

12

13

0   10   20m

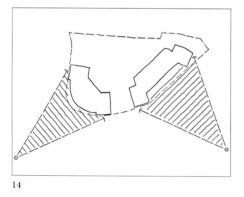

14

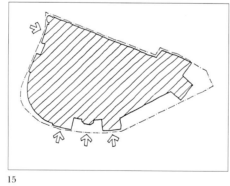

15

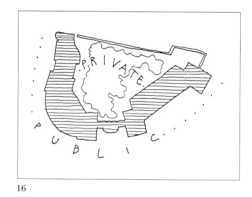

16

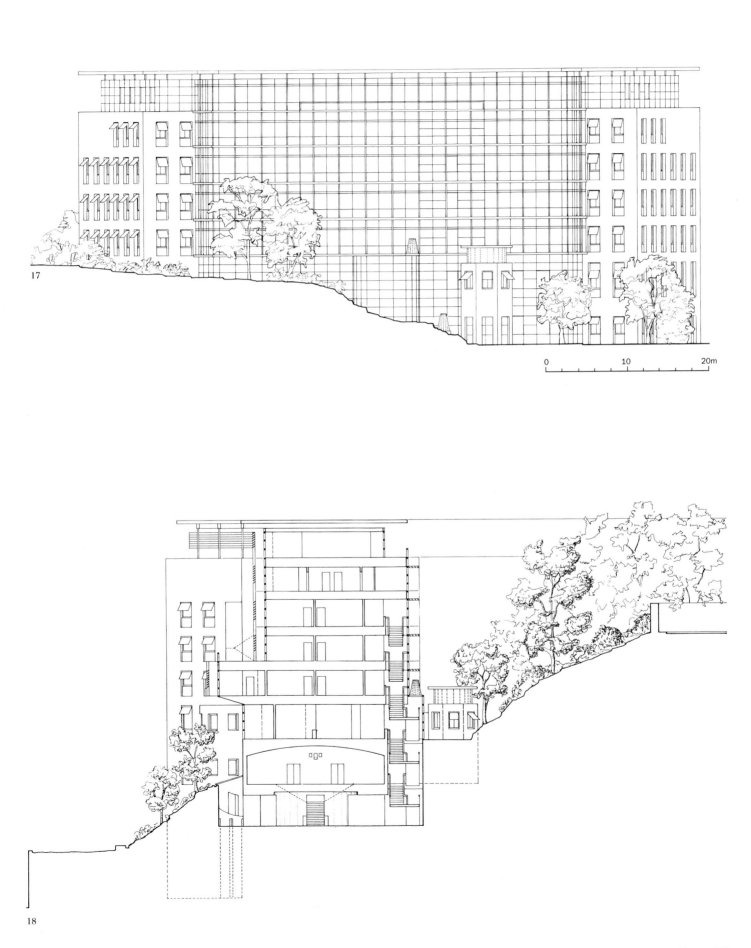

17

18

19

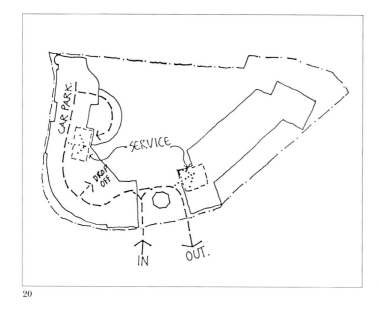

20

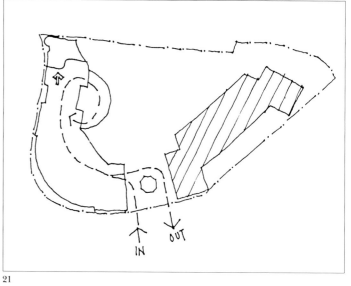

21

19 Model: east elevation, the British Consulate-General Headquarters
20 Conceptual study: vehicular access
21 Conceptual study: residential access
22 Model: view of north elevation

22

Sainsbury's Supermarket

Design/Completion 1992/1994
Fourth and Fifth Avenue, Harlow, Essex
J Sainsbury PLC
70,000 square feet (building only); site area: 9.5 acres (including parking)
Steel frame; concrete slabs on metal decking
Architectural masonry; flat and profiled metal cladding;
structural glazing; render; membrane roof

The proposals for a new supermarket on a nine-acre site adjoining Harlow Town Centre are based on urban design principles. The scheme comprises a store, car parking, and a new petrol filling station. Access is from a new roundabout and section of dual carriageway, with separate service access off the existing northern boundary road. The proposed site layout relates strongly to the context. The store is located in the north-west corner, adjacent to an existing mature woodland. Parking is divided into two main areas crossed by axial routes relating the store entrance to the site perimeter. The entrance is treated as a collection of individual components linked to the main building, clearly visible at the heart of the site. Along the northern boundary, the building steps down to meet the adjoining road, and staff accommodation below the main sales level animates the existing faceless retaining wall.

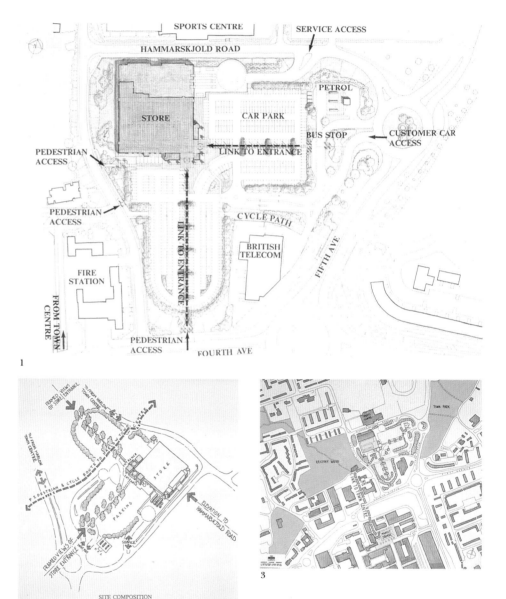

1

2 SITE COMPOSITION

3

1 Site layout
2 Site composition study
3 Context plan
4 Master plan model: aerial view towards
  town centre
5 Master plan model: aerial view of store entrance
  from the east
6 Site layout plan

196

4

5

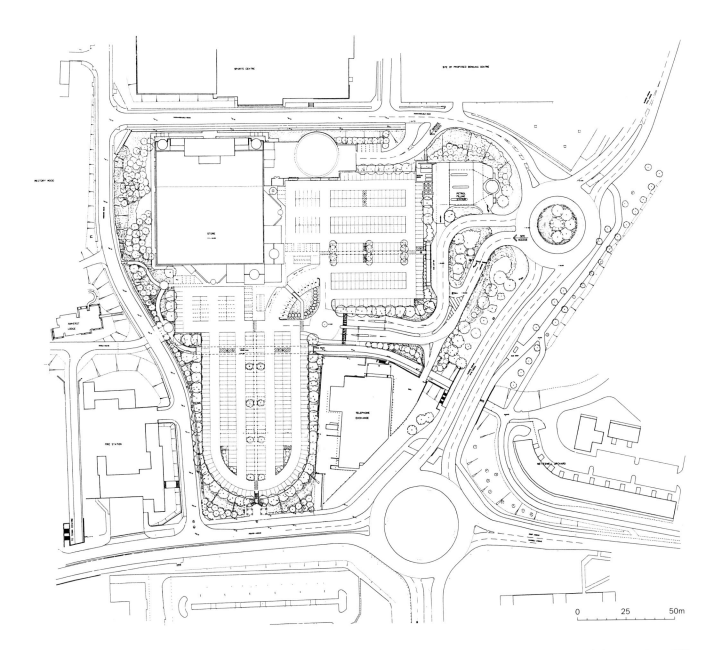

6

7　Shopfront entrance: isometric projection viewed from above
8　Shopfront entrance: isometric projection viewed from below
9　Hammarskjold Road elevation: north and south views isometric projection viewed from above
10　Shopfront entrance glazed canopy and revolving door: isometric view from below
11　Colour model studies of the store entrance
12　Colour model studies from the north-east

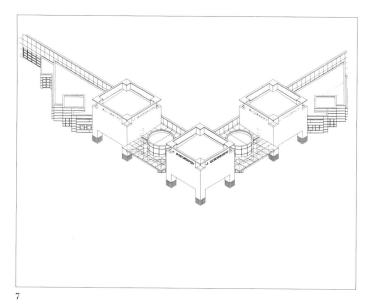

7

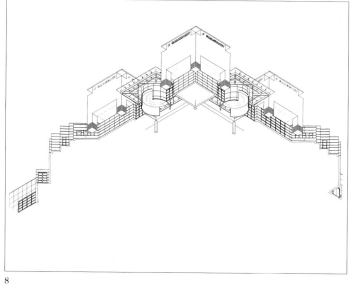

8

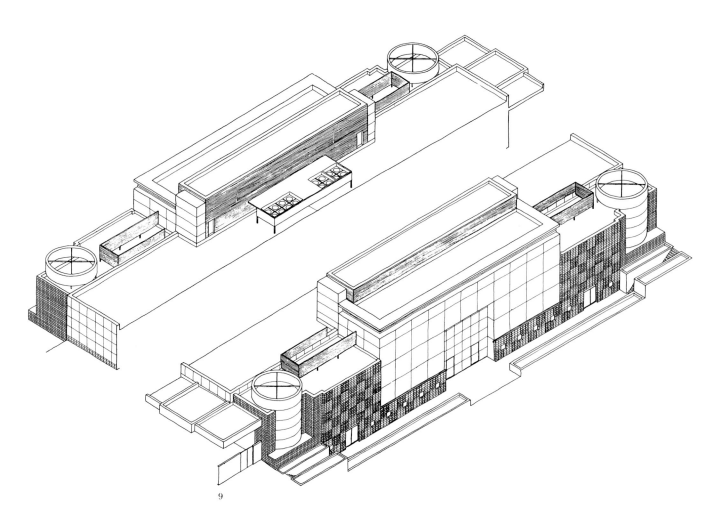

9

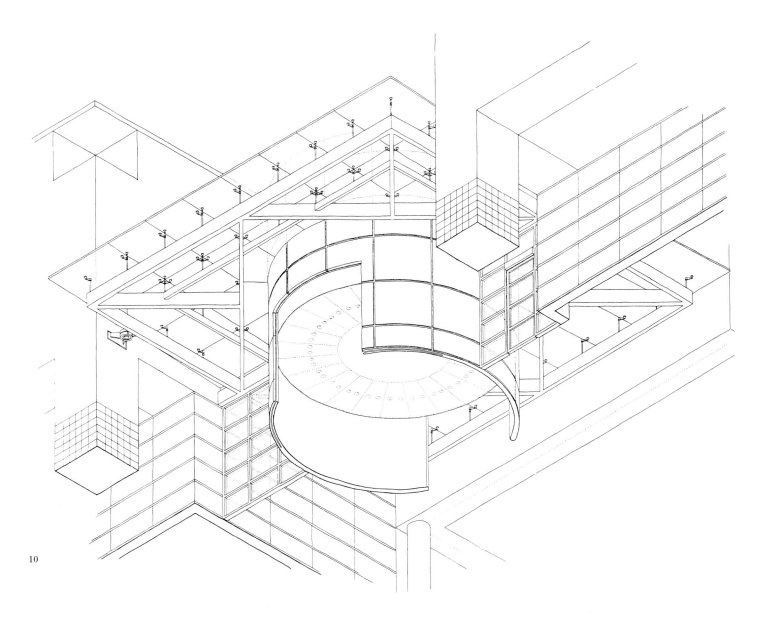

10

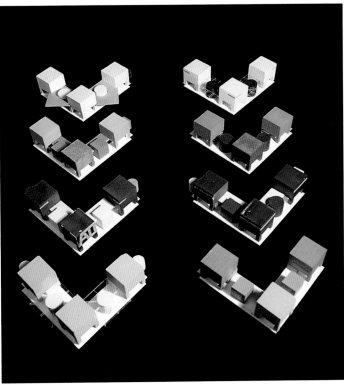

11

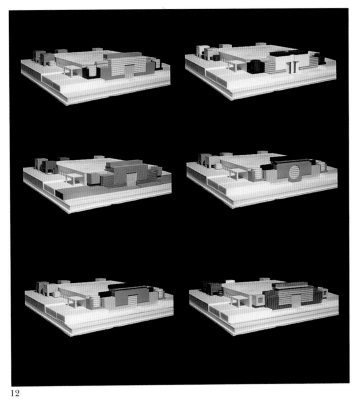

12

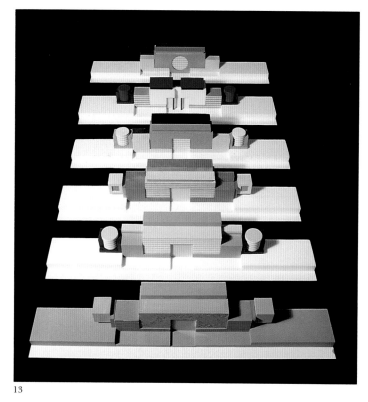

13

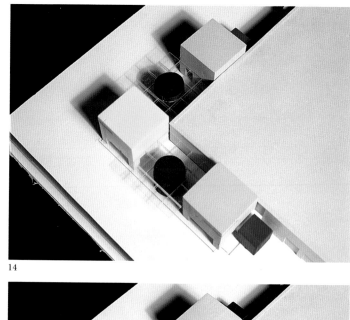

14

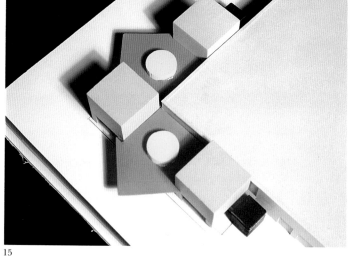

15

13 Colour model studies
14 Colour model study of the store entrance
15 Colour model study of the store entrance
16 Colour model studies of the main entrance

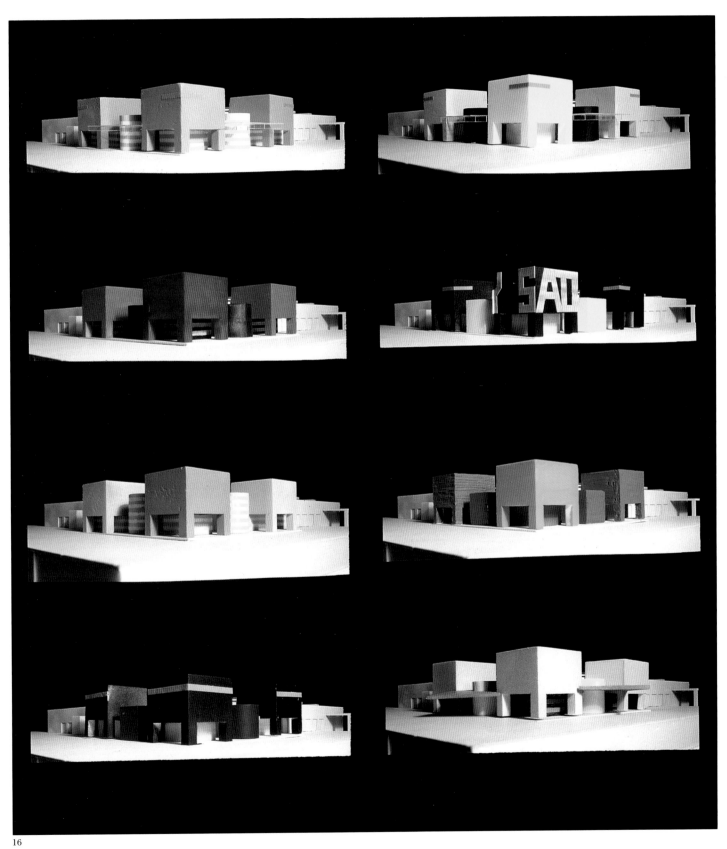

Braehead Retail Complex

Design/Completion 1993
Glasgow
Competition organised by J Sainsbury PLC and Marks & Spencer
Single-level scheme: 122,764 square feet
Two-level scheme: 225,805 square feet
Steel structural frame and either reinforced concrete in situ or concrete plank floors together with a single membrane flat roof finish laid on a deck
Metal frame and lightweight tensile web infill canopy; stainless steel coping and fixings; stack bonded masonry blockwork; colour coated metal frame windows and doors; ceramic cladding; metal and glass or 'Planar' glass canopy: colour acrylic render with recessed V-joints

This scheme included a 600,000-square-foot shopping centre and 150,000 square feet of leisure and restaurant space, a business park, retail warehouse and a hotel. A master plan approach was adopted to unify the site and to create an identity for a neglected and derelict location. A framework or "grid" layout with key locations identified by bold colours and forms, orientates and directs the shopper around the site. The planning of the shopping centre itself is on the traditional "dumbbell" principle, with clear visual links between "anchor" stores, and food court, restaurant and leisure facilities located at an equal distance between them. Entrances are strategically located to promote pedestrian circulation through the complex, and car parking is evenly distributed around the building in well-screened avenues of mature trees.

The approach to the landscape is based on contrasts between abstract shapes and natural forms, so that familiar elements become surprising, thus introducing an element of fantasy.

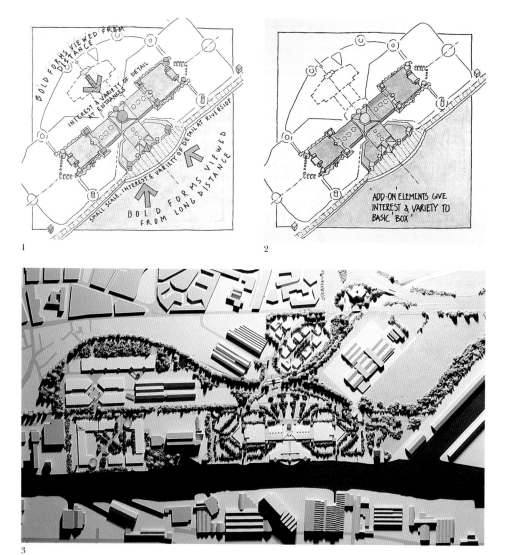

1

2

3

1   Concept sketch: views
2   Concept sketch: add-on elements
3   Aerial of master plan model
4   North-west/south-east section
5   North-east/south-west section
6   Aerial perspective
7   Eye-level study of entrance to major stores
8   Eye-level study of entrance to major stores

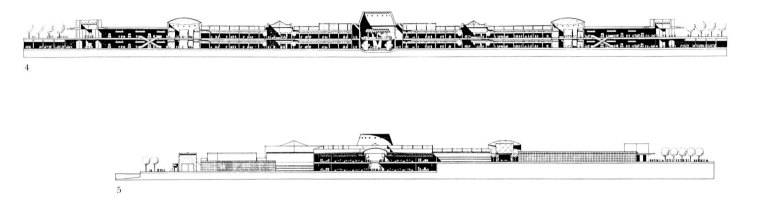

4

5

6

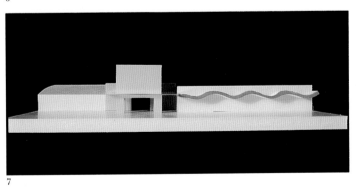

7

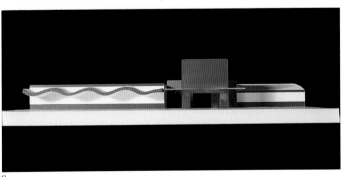

8

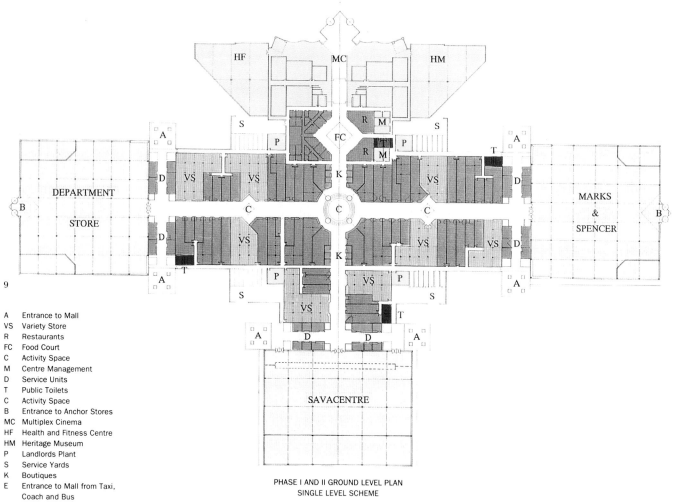

E

HF MC HM

S R M S

FC

P T M P

A A

T

D VS VS K VS D

B C C C B

DEPARTMENT   MARKS
                        &
STORE   SPENCER

D VS K VS VS D

A A

T

P VS P

S S

9

A   Entrance to Mall   VS T
VS Variety Store
R   Restaurants   A D D A
FC Food Court
C   Activity Space
M   Centre Management
D   Service Units
T   Public Toilets
C   Activity Space   SAVACENTRE
B   Entrance to Anchor Stores
MC Multiplex Cinema
HF Health and Fitness Centre
HM Heritage Museum
P   Landlords Plant
S   Service Yards
K   Boutiques   PHASE I AND II GROUND LEVEL PLAN
E   Entrance to Mall from Taxi,   SINGLE LEVEL SCHEME
    Coach and Bus

9 Phase I and phase II ground-level plan: single-level scheme
10 Study model: perspective view of leisure element
11 Study model: perspective view of leisure element along the river frontage
12 Study model: building 2
13 Study model: store and entrance gateways
14 Study model: building 1

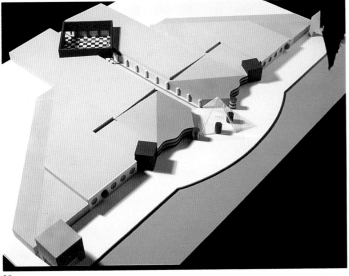

10

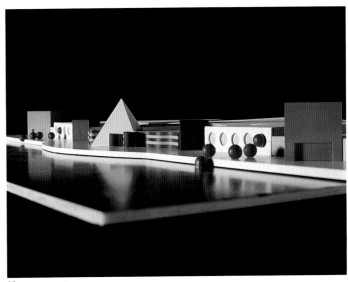

11

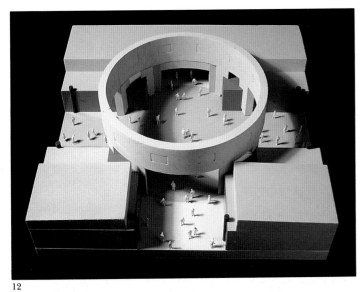

12

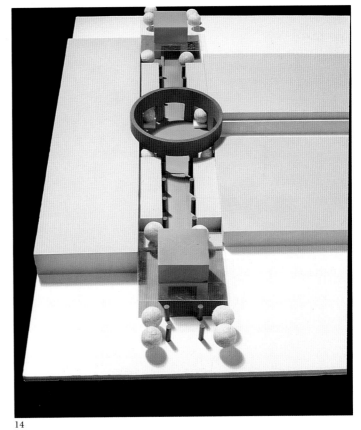

14

13

Kowloon Station, Hong Kong

Design/Completion 1992/1997
Kowloon, Hong Kong
Mass Transit Railway Corporation
Station building: 1,735,000 square feet
Master plan area: 11,000,000 square feet
Reinforced concrete generally; steel for principal concourse roof
Metal and glass cladding; stainless steel standing seam roof
to concourse; granite and terrazzo tiles internally

Kowloon Station will be a major transport interchange on the new rail-link included in MTRC's proposals for the connection of Hong Kong Central and the new airport at Chek Lap Kok. The design provides for interchange between three separate rail lines; airport check-in; and coach, bus and road transport, linked by a mezzanine concourse. It also includes the urban design master plan for air-rights development over and around the station, consisting of 11,000,000 square feet of mixed hotel, office, retail and residential space organised around three public squares, which will be the focus for the development. In the centre of each is a large conservatory. These connect the station and air-rights building, bring the garden environment into the mezzanine concourse and daylight into the station, and form the entrances to the station from the podium. The scheme will provide a focus for the development of a new city district being reclaimed in the west of Kowloon.

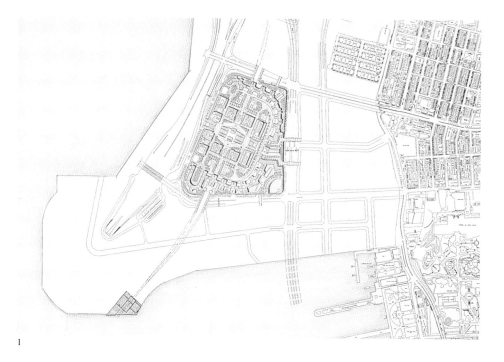

1

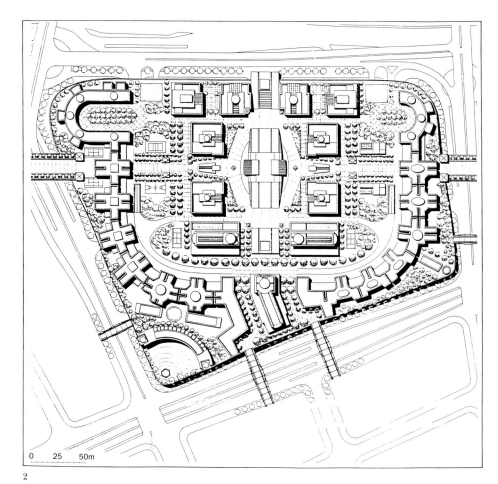

0   25   50m

2

STATION PLOT

STATION & MASTERPLAN
INTEGRATION

RETAIL SPACE

PEDESTRIAN LINKS

3

VIEWS

BREEZEWAY

RESIDENTIAL TOWERS

PUBLIC SPACE

RESIDENTIAL MIX

MASTERPLAN USES

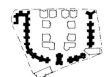

HOTELS

PHASING

PEDESTRIAN LINKS

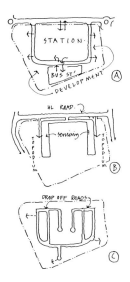

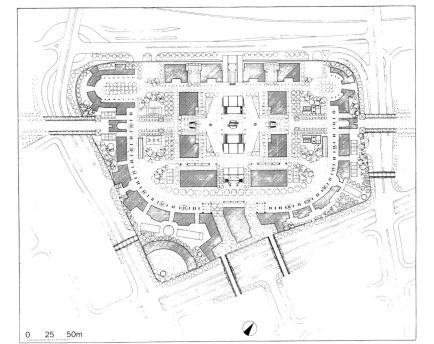

0   25   50m

4

1   Kowloon Station and Kowloon Ventilation
    Building location plan
2   Master plan
3   Master plan concept diagrams
4   Podium-level plan

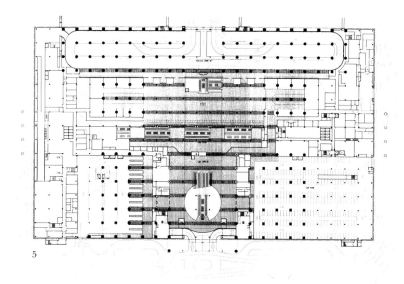

5

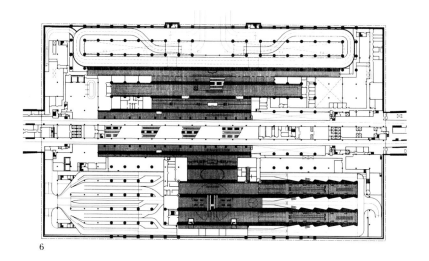

6

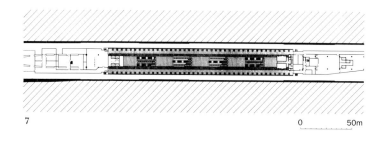

7

0   50m

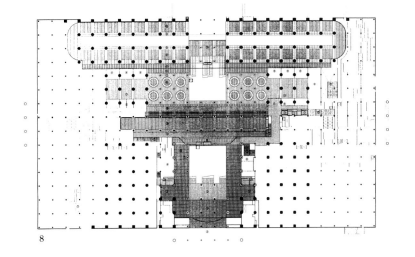

8

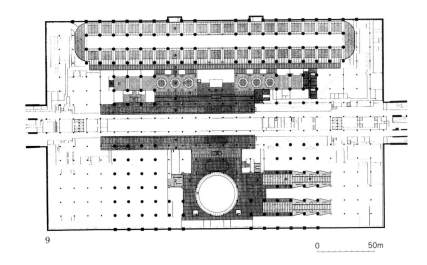

9

0   50m

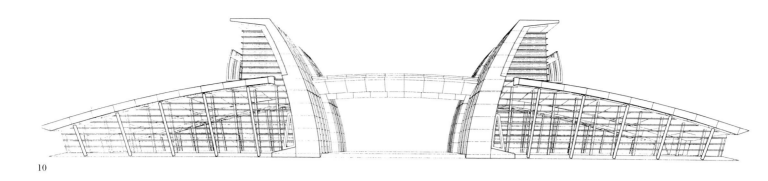

10

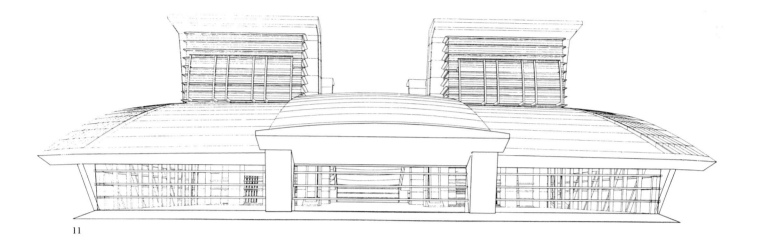

11

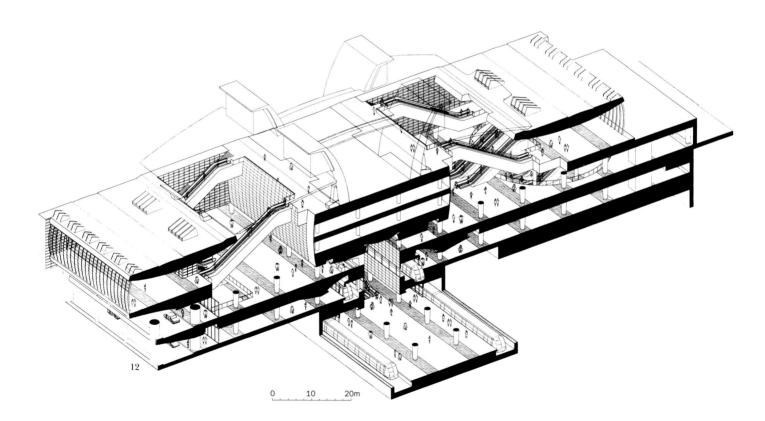

12

0   10   20m

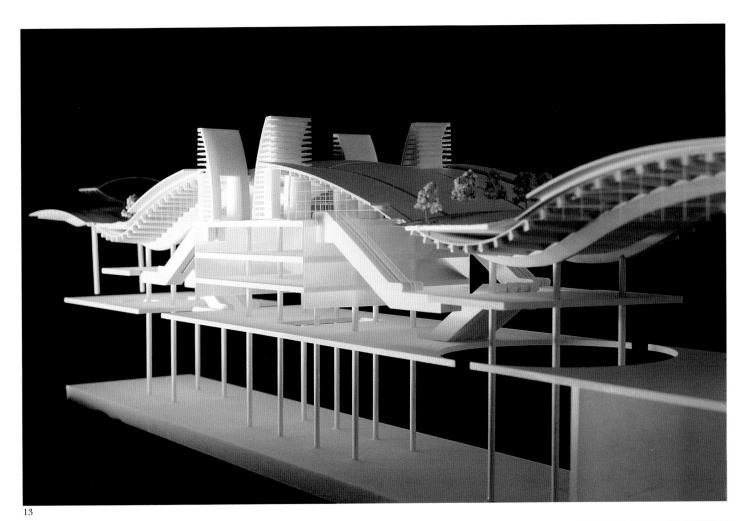

13

14

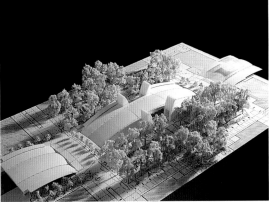

15

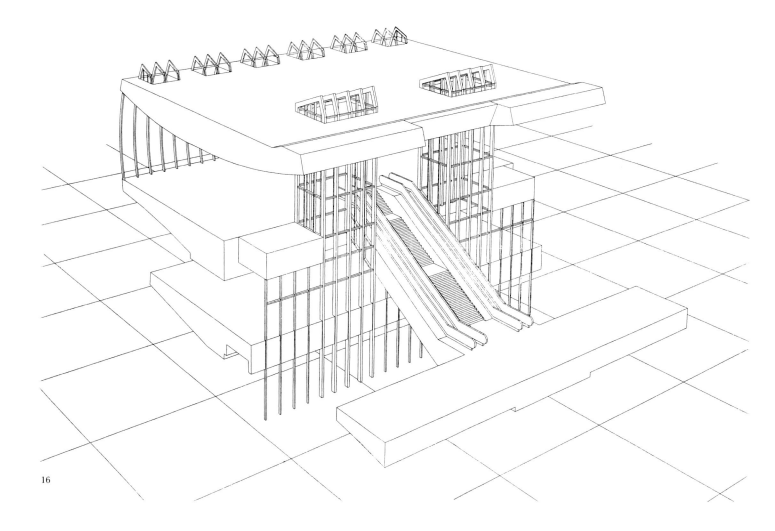

16

17

18

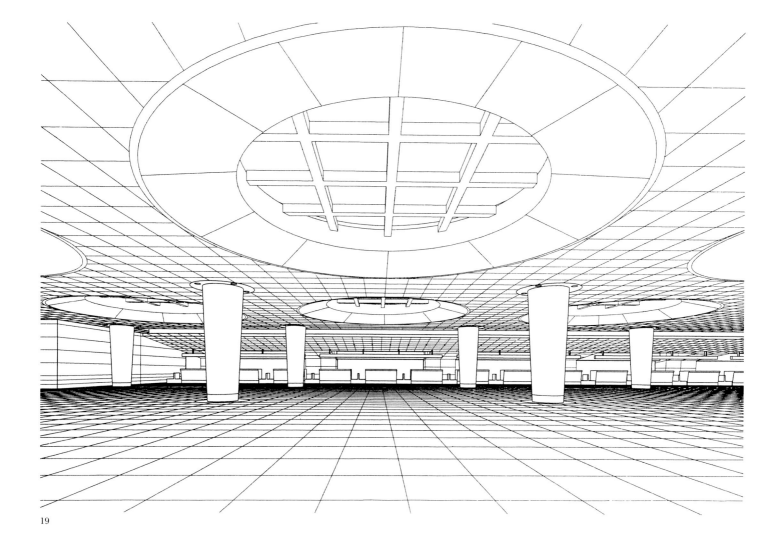

19

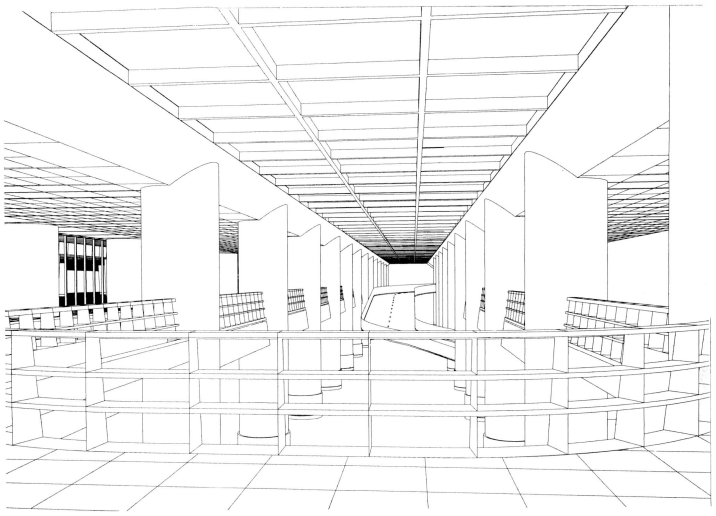

20

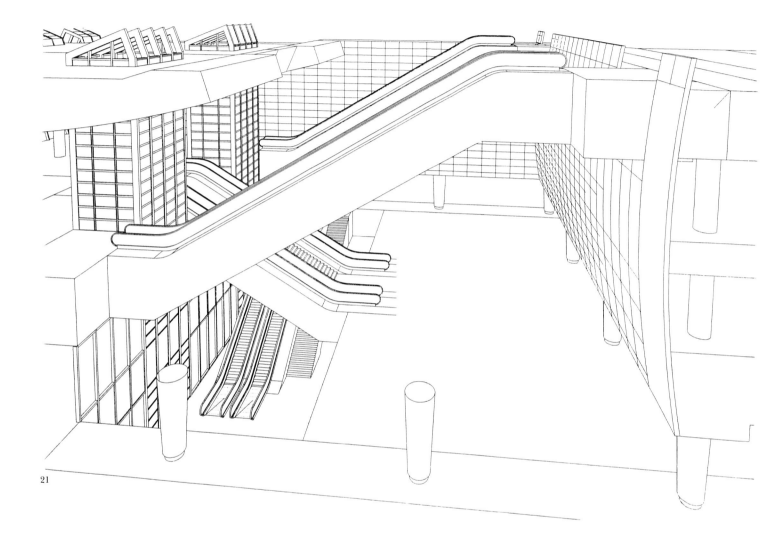

21 Axonometric of lightwells and entrance escalators
22 Station roof model: north-east elevation, illuminated
23 Station roof model: facing south, master plan buildings in background
24 Station roof model: detail

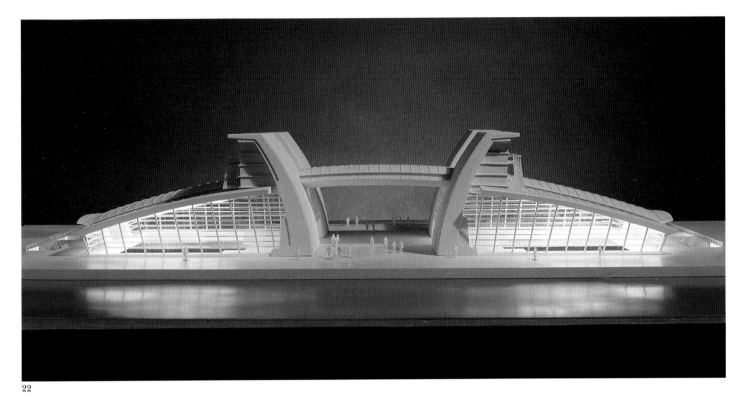

22

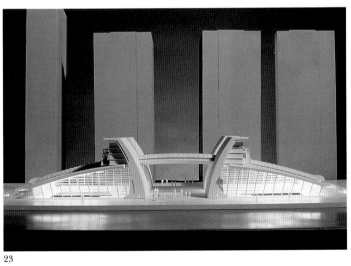

23

24

Fort Canning Radio Tower, Singapore

Design/Completion 1992
Singapore
Competition organised by Singapore Telecom
32,500 square feet
Structural steel mast with radio-transparent cable stays; reinforced concrete floors; reinforced concrete core; prestressed ties, comprising multi-core steel ties, encased in concrete with steel over sleeves; reinforced concrete basement
Fabricated high grade steel mast; laminated glass screens; glazed panels; PVF^2 louvre panels; PVF^2 coated aluminium panels; stonework finishes at ground level

The competition brief set out requirements for a telecommunication tower which will rank among the tallest in the world. It is to be constructed on a restricted site on a prominent hillside commanding wide views of surrounding areas, including Singapore city. The design challenge was to find an elegant solution which would have a strong public image, both at close quarters and from far away, and be an intelligent and adaptable communications facility consistent with the functional requirements and sensitive nature of its position within a landscaped park. Our proposals were submitted for the competition and won third place.

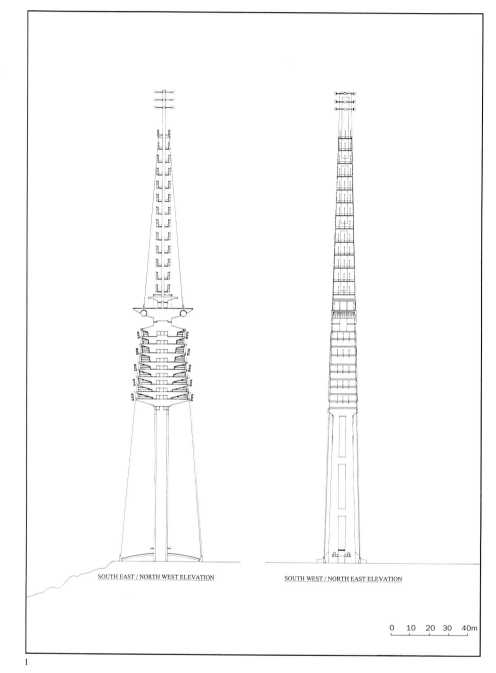

SOUTH EAST / NORTH WEST ELEVATION   SOUTH WEST / NORTH EAST ELEVATION

0   10   20   30   40m

1

1 Left: south-east/north-west elevation
   Right: south-west/north-east elevation
2 Original scheme model
3 Original scheme model
4 Original scheme model
5 Perspective view

2

3

4

5

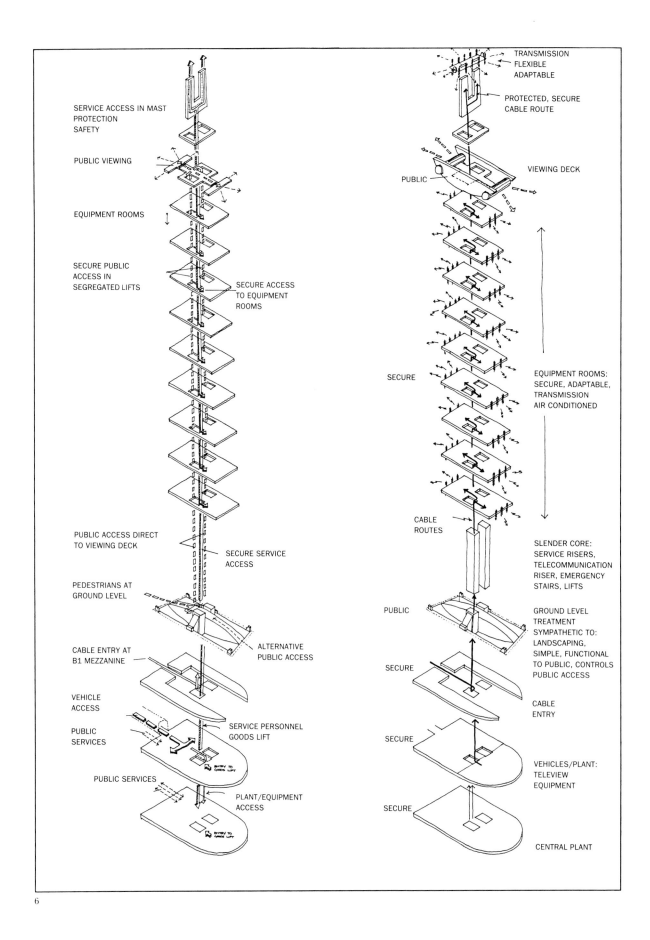

SERVICE ACCESS IN MAST
PROTECTION
SAFETY

PUBLIC VIEWING

EQUIPMENT ROOMS

SECURE PUBLIC
ACCESS IN
SEGREGATED LIFTS

SECURE ACCESS
TO EQUIPMENT
ROOMS

PUBLIC ACCESS DIRECT
TO VIEWING DECK

SECURE SERVICE
ACCESS

PEDESTRIANS AT
GROUND LEVEL

CABLE ENTRY AT
B1 MEZZANINE

ALTERNATIVE
PUBLIC ACCESS

VEHICLE
ACCESS

PUBLIC
SERVICES

SERVICE PERSONNEL
GOODS LIFT

ENTRY TO GOODS LIFT

PUBLIC SERVICES

PLANT/EQUIPMENT
ACCESS

ENTRY TO GOODS LIFT

TRANSMISSION
FLEXIBLE
ADAPTABLE

PROTECTED, SECURE
CABLE ROUTE

PUBLIC

VIEWING DECK

SECURE

EQUIPMENT ROOMS:
SECURE, ADAPTABLE,
TRANSMISSION
AIR CONDITIONED

CABLE
ROUTES

SLENDER CORE:
SERVICE RISERS,
TELECOMMUNICATION
RISER, EMERGENCY
STAIRS, LIFTS

PUBLIC

GROUND LEVEL
TREATMENT
SYMPATHETIC TO:
LANDSCAPING,
SIMPLE, FUNCTIONAL
TO PUBLIC, CONTROLS
PUBLIC ACCESS

SECURE

CABLE
ENTRY

SECURE

VEHICLES/PLANT:
TELEVIEW
EQUIPMENT

SECURE

CENTRAL PLANT

6

7

8

6   Vehicle and pedestrian traffic flow: functional flow chart
7   Updated model
8   Updated model
9   Updated model

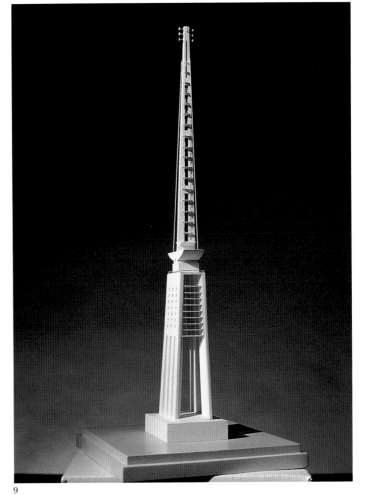

9

New National Gallery of Scottish Art and History

Design/Completion 1993/1994
Kelvingrove Park, Glasgow, Scotland
Study for the Glasgow Development Agency in conjunction with Glasgow
Museums and the Scottish National Galleries
97,000 square feet (gallery building)
Precast concrete driven piles; reinforced concrete water-tight construction
ground floors; waffle slab upper floors; steelwork truss
Lightweight roof decking and glazing units; steelwork trusses

In February 1993 Terry Farrell was invited
by the Glasgow Development Agency to
put forward a vision for the new National
Gallery of Scottish Art and History in
Kelvingrove Park that would reflect the
vigour, variety and invention
of Scottish art and culture. The gallery
will embrace the evolving tradition of
Scottish art from its beginnings to the
present day. Changing exhibitions and
a complete library of the history of
Scottish art will create an environment
in which the general public and scholars
alike can appreciate and study Scotland's
national heritage.

The proposals for the new gallery,
in harmony with the park landscape,
Kelvingrove Art Gallery & Museum and
the University of Glasgow, will revive
the historic role of the park as Glasgow's
major site for arts festivals and other
major cultural events.

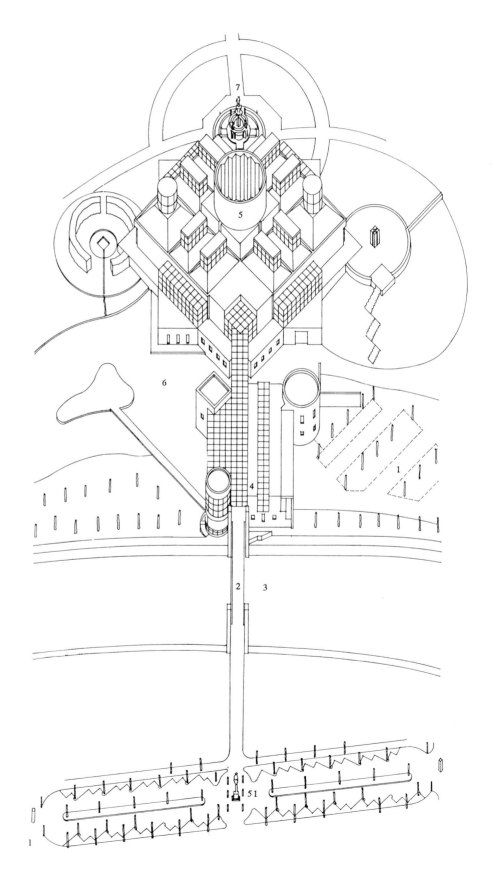

1   Building elements
2   Master plan

222

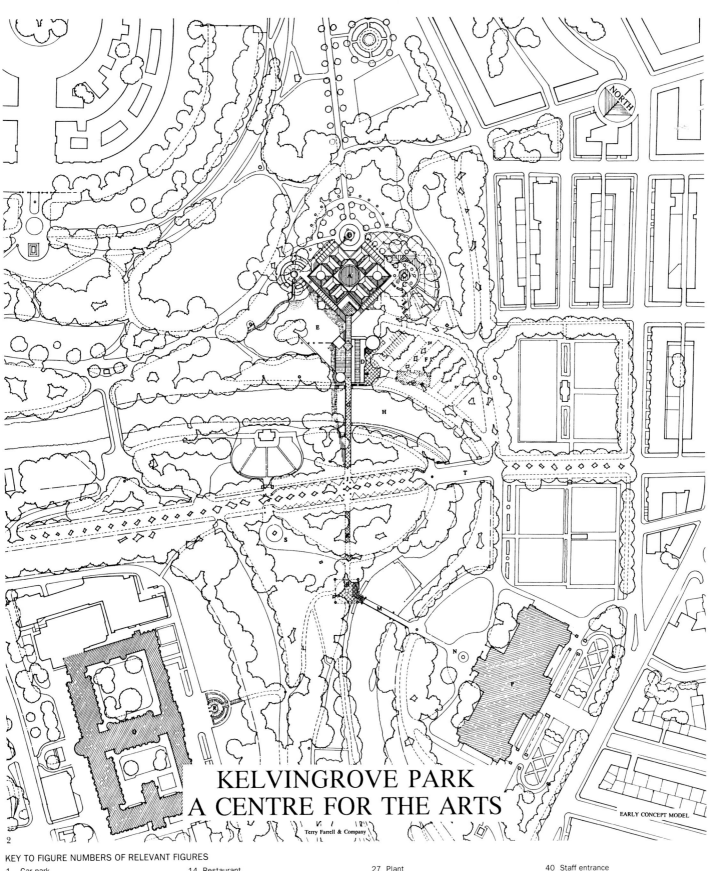

KELVINGROVE PARK
A CENTRE FOR THE ARTS

Terry Farrell & Company

EARLY CONCEPT MODEL

KEY TO FIGURE NUMBERS OF RELEVANT FIGURES

1	Car park	14	Restaurant	27	Plant	40	Staff entrance
2	New bridge	15	Artist's studio	28	Reserve galleries	41	Toilets
3	River Kelvin	16	Female toilets	29	Handling area	42	Reception and cloakroom
4	Entrance building	17	Male toilets	30	Art lift	43	Lecture theatre
5	Gallery building	18	Education rooms	31	Conservation workshop and studio	44	Backstage/changing room/projection room
6	Lake	19	Shop	32	Handling workshop	45	Seminar room
7	Stewart Memorial fountain	20	Entry and orientation area	33	Conservation offices	46	Ramp to gallery level
8	Galleries	21	Ramp from car-park level	34	Warder's accommodation	47	Sculpture galleries
9	Sculpture galleries	22	Library	35	Loading bay	48	Sculpture terraces
10	Sculpture terraces	23	Drawings and prints	36	Lakeside terrace	49	Sculpture courts
11	Entrance	24	Reference	37	Kitchen	49	Stewart Memorial fountain
12	Art lift	25	Photographic archive	38	Curatorial accommodation	50	Car parking
13	Board room	26	Display for prints, drawings and photographs	39	Artist's studio		

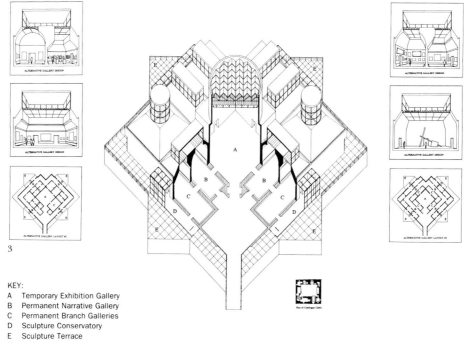

3

KEY:
A   Temporary Exhibition Gallery
B   Permanent Narrative Gallery
C   Permanent Branch Galleries
D   Sculpture Conservatory
E   Sculpture Terrace

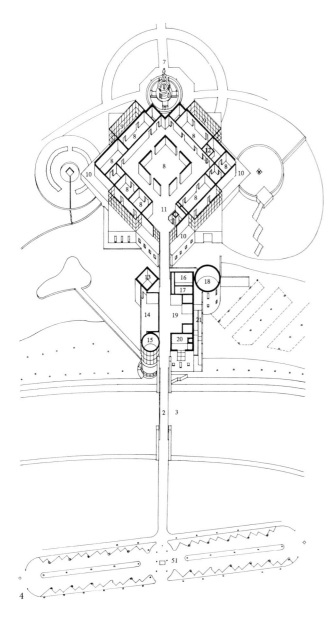

4

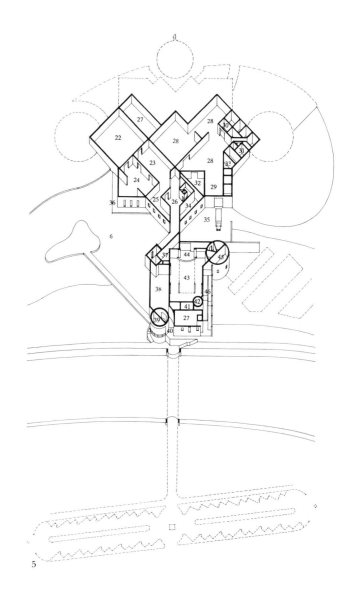

5

3 Axonometric of galleries
4 Upper ground-floor plan
5 Lower ground-floor plan
6 Model: detail of gallery, illuminated
7 Aerial perspective
8 Alternative gallery designs

6

7

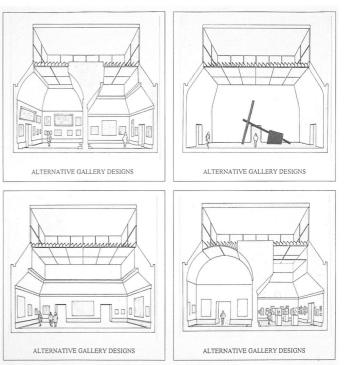

ALTERNATIVE GALLERY DESIGNS

ALTERNATIVE GALLERY DESIGNS

ALTERNATIVE GALLERY DESIGNS

ALTERNATIVE GALLERY DESIGNS

8

9   Model: aerial view
10 Model: detail
11 View approaching the building from the south-east,
    with the Stewart Memorial fountain
12 Model

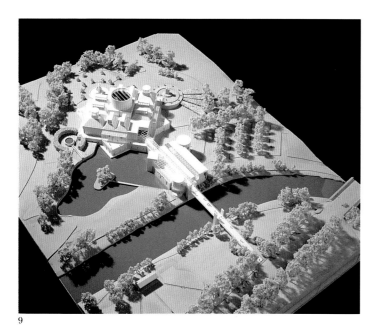

9

10

11

12

Kowloon Ventilation Building, Hong Kong

Design/Completion 1993/1997
Kowloon, Hong Kong
Mass Transit Railway Corporation
95,620 square feet
Reinforced concrete
Profiled aluminium cladding; ceramic tile and mosaic

The KVB is one of a series of ancillary buildings containing mechanical and electrical equipment along the length of the proposed airport rail-link. It contains floodgates, power transformers and ventilation units, and sits in a large public park overlooking the harbour. Because of the prominence of the site, a landmark building of high quality was required. It will be visually strong but also sympathetic to its setting, an organic design with undulating form relating to banks of rolling landscape and waves of the harbour. The surrounding landscape and harbourscape will be designed to echo and enhance the shape of the building, which will be completed in early 1997.

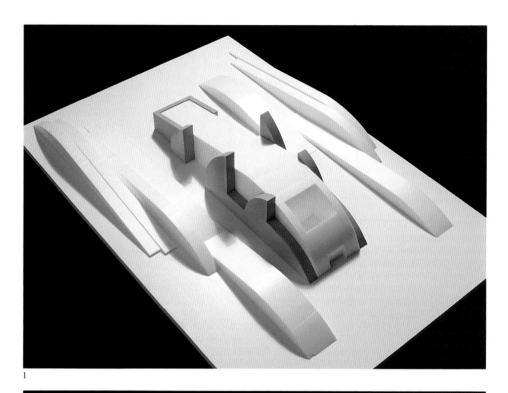

1

2

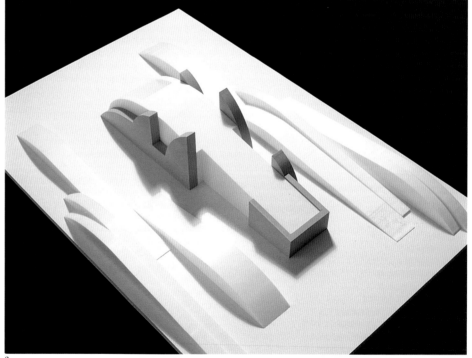

3

1 Study model
2 Conceptual sketch
3 Study model
4 Ground-level plan
5 Level 1A and level 1 plan
6 Colour study models
7 Longitudinal section

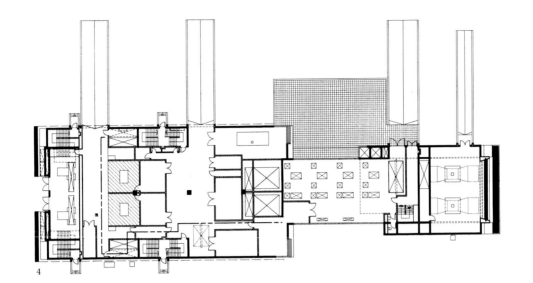

4

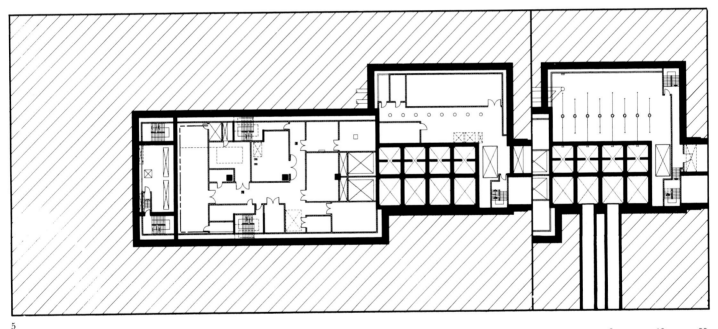

5

0   10   20m

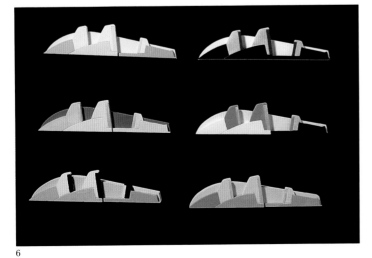

6

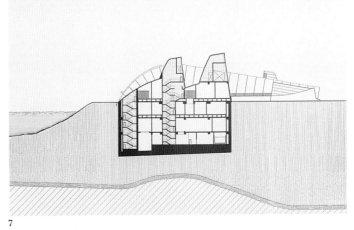

7

Kowloon Ventilation Building, Hong Kong   229

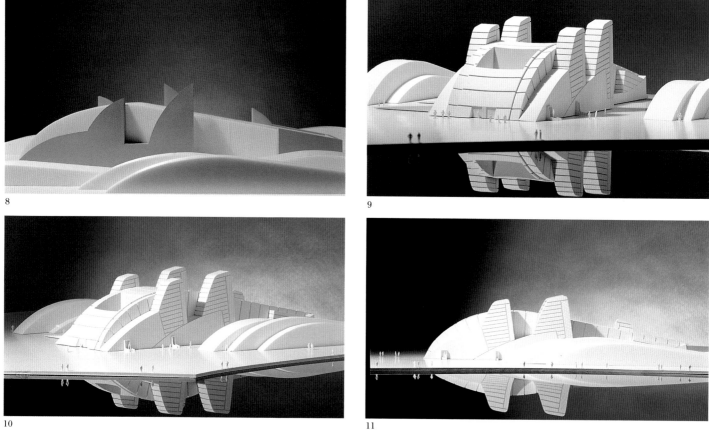

8

9

10

11

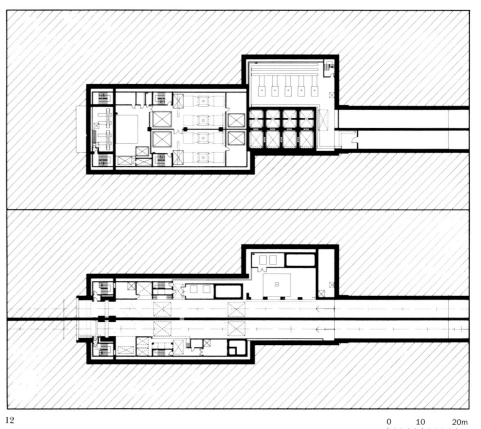

8   Study model
9   Model: south elevation over harbour
10 Model: east elevation over harbour
11 Model: east elevation
12 Top: level 0 plan
    Bottom: track-level plan
13 Longitudinal section, with railway track
14 Roof-level plan
15 Level 3 plan
16 Cross section

12

0   10   20m

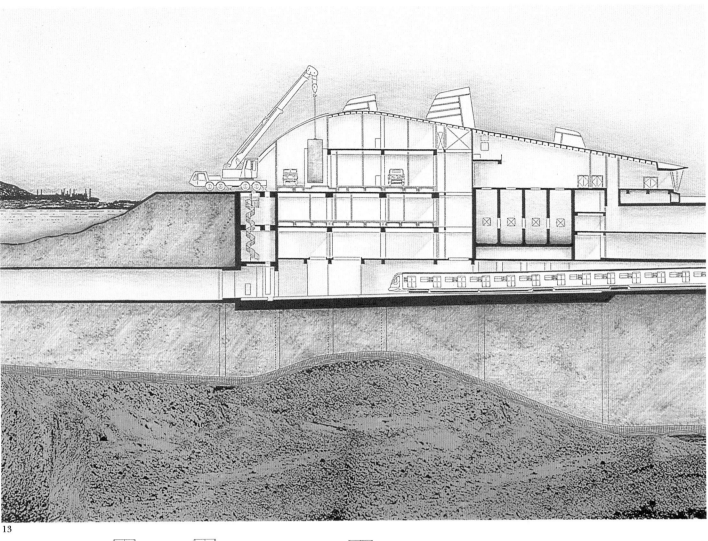

13

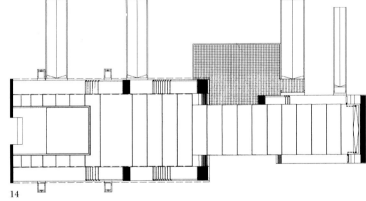

14

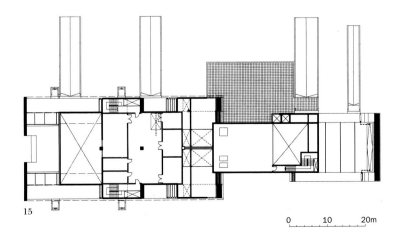

15

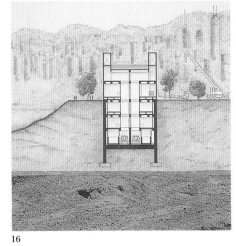

16

0   10   20m

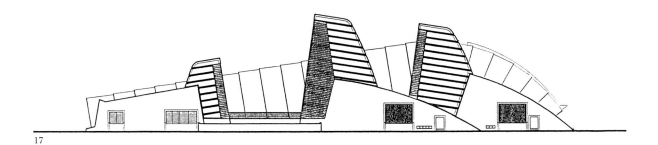

17

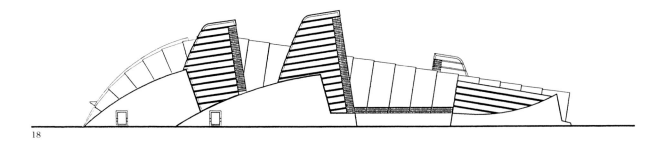

18

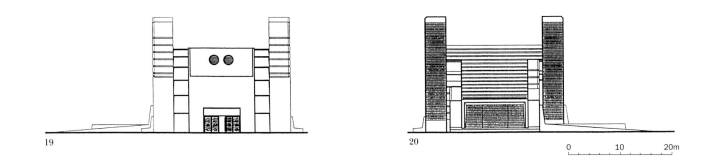

19   20

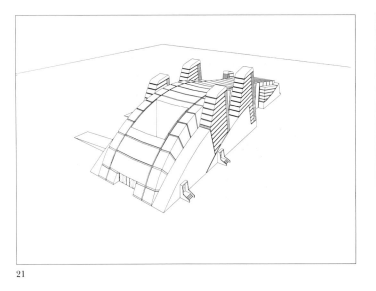

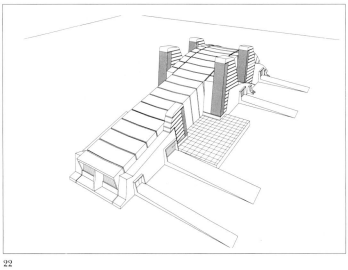

21   22

23

Library and Culture Centre, Dubai

Design/Completion 1993/1996
Dubai
Competition organised by UNESCO for a private sponsor
277,000 square feet
Structural steelwork "trees"; reinforced concrete walls and slabs
Marble and terrazzo floors; marble walls with timber panelwork and
plaster ceilings; steel column "trees" with granite base cladding;
glazed screens; anodised aluminium external supports and glazing frames

The design aims to provide an appropriate and inspiring environment for the collection and preparation of material relating to the spiritual and cultural heritage of the region and the Islamic and Arab world, serving scholars, students, professionals and the general public.

The architecture of the complex integrates traditional forms and layouts with modern forms and structure. The scheme derives from an "urban" idea of a collection of buildings and spaces, rather than a conventional western idea of a library and cultural centre as an institution or single civic building. The library is interpreted as an enclosed space, focused on a central pavilion of knowledge. The Culture Centre is interpreted as a composition of defining forms accommodating different functions around a courtyard (void), at the centre of which is a pool representing the association of water and spirituality. These two elements are positioned around a central axis, with pedestrian access from the north and service access from the south.

1

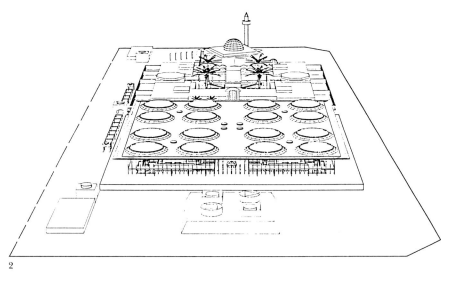

2

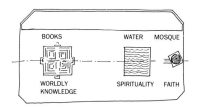

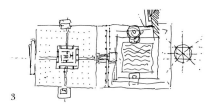

3

1 Axial view towards library across courtyard of Culture Centre
2 Aerial view of the complete project
3 Conceptual sketches
4 Longitudinal section through the entrance hall
5 East elevation
6 Cross section through the library

BAZAAR   OPEN COURTYARD   CENTRAL HALL   SPECIAL COLLECTIONS

4

CAFETERIA PRAYER ROOM   BAZAAR   CHILDREN'S LIBRARY   HEAT REJECTION PLANT

5

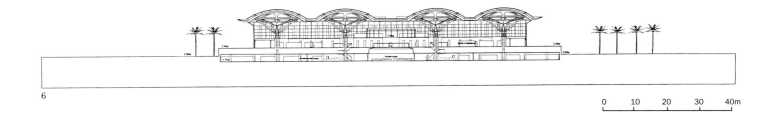

6

0   10   20   30   40m

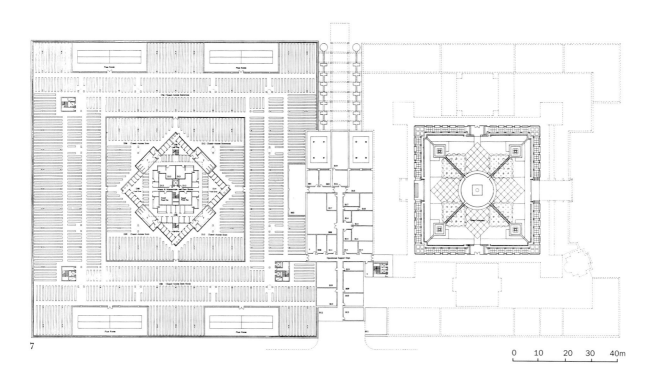

7

0 10 20 30 40m

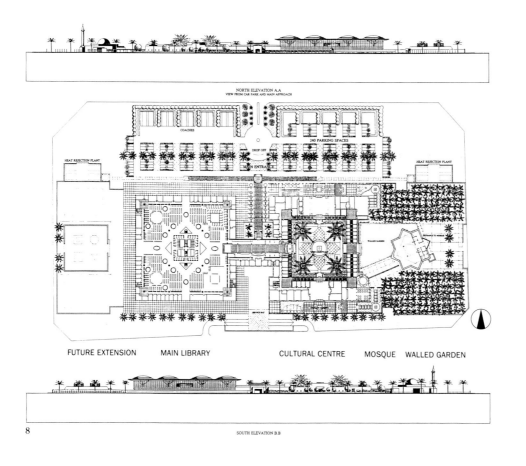

NORTH ELEVATION A.A
VIEW FROM CAR PARK AND MAIN APPROACH

FUTURE EXTENSION   MAIN LIBRARY   CULTURAL CENTRE   MOSQUE   WALLED GARDEN

8   SOUTH ELEVATION B.B

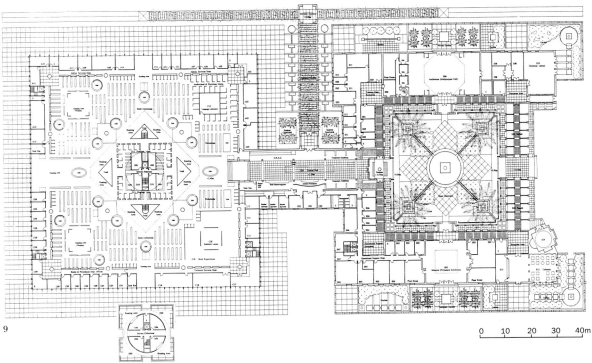

9

0 10 20 30 40m

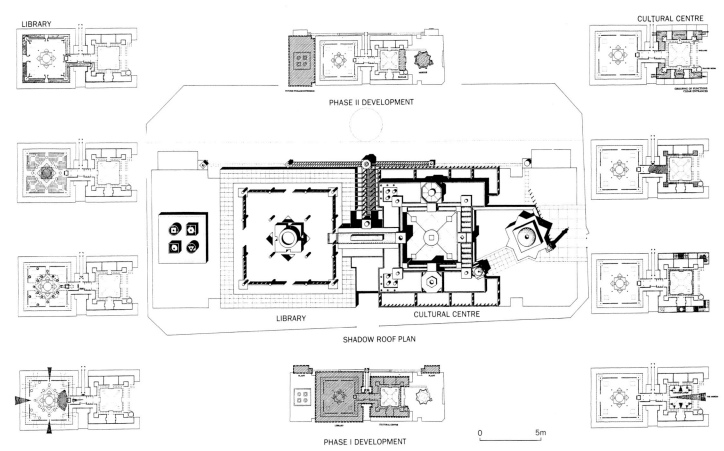

LIBRARY

PHASE II DEVELOPMENT

CULTURAL CENTRE

GROUPING OF FUNCTIONS
CLEAR ENTRANCES

SHADOW ROOF PLAN

LIBRARY

CULTURAL CENTRE

PHASE I DEVELOPMENT

0 5m

10

11 Reflected ceiling plan
12 Building analysis (left to right): (a)sun path and shading; (b)walls and
  pavilions; (c)the garden and the courtyard; (d)pedestrian movements:
  ground level; (e)book movements: lower-ground level
13 Environmental response of library envelope
14 Integration of structure and air distribution

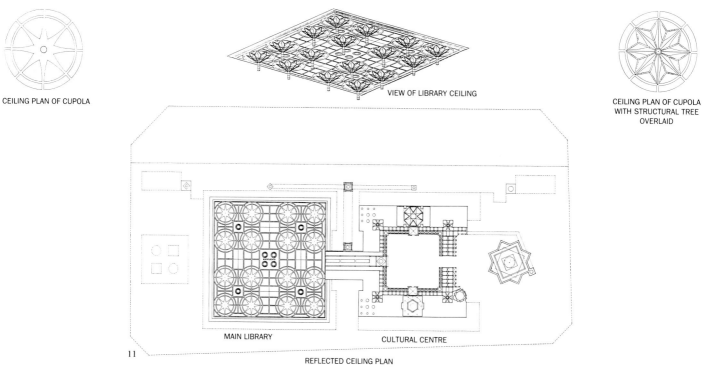

CEILING PLAN OF CUPOLA

VIEW OF LIBRARY CEILING

CEILING PLAN OF CUPOLA
WITH STRUCTURAL TREE
OVERLAID

MAIN LIBRARY

CULTURAL CENTRE

11

REFLECTED CEILING PLAN

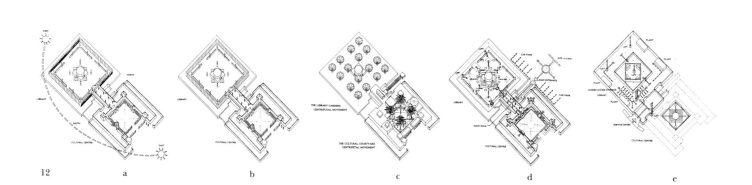

12   a   b   c   d   e

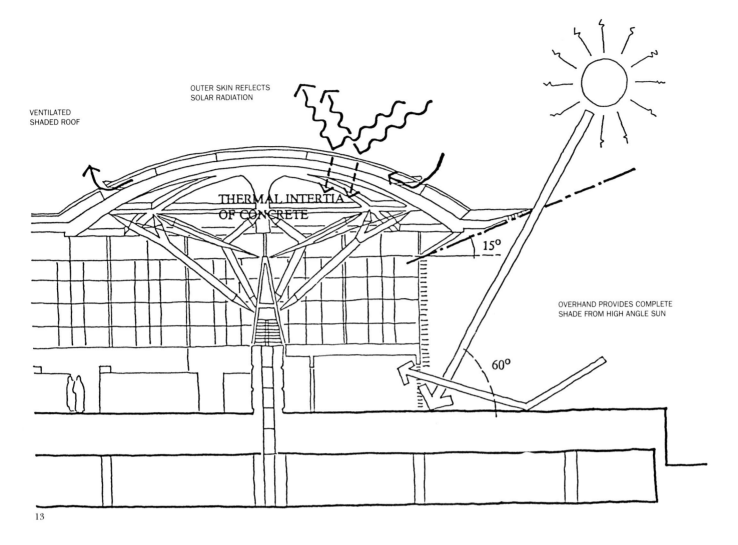

OUTER SKIN REFLECTS
SOLAR RADIATION

VENTILATED
SHADED ROOF

THERMAL INTERTIA
OF CONCRETE

15°

OVERHAND PROVIDES COMPLETE
SHADE FROM HIGH ANGLE SUN

60°

13

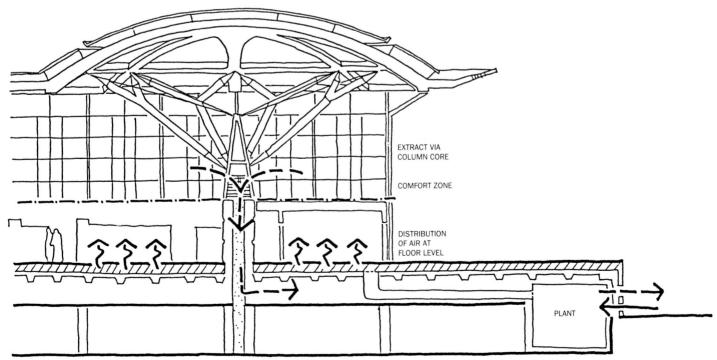

EXTRACT VIA
COLUMN CORE

COMFORT ZONE

DISTRIBUTION
OF AIR AT
FLOOR LEVEL

PLANT

14

Firm Profile

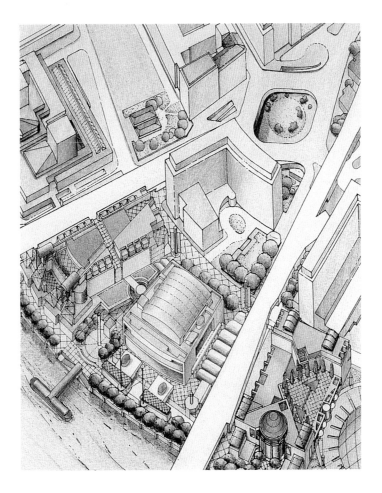

Biographies

TERRY FARRELL
OBE, MCP, MRTPI, RIBA, FSCD, M.Arch., RIBA

Terry Farrell was born on 12 May 1938 near Manchester, England. He grew up in Newcastle upon Tyne and attended the University of Newcastle School of Architecture from 1956 to 1961, where he received a Bachelor of Architecture Degree with First Class Honours. He went as a Harkness Fellow to the University of Pennsylvania from 1962 to 1964, a time when the tutors included Louis Kahn, Romaldo Giurgola, Bob Venturi and Denise Scott Brown, and graduated with Masters Degrees in Architecture and City Planning. During this period he travelled extensively in America and subsequently won two study scholarships which enabled him to make a study tour of government housing and town planning in Japan. Terry Farrell worked briefly for the Planning Department, Camden, New Jersey, USA and then for Colin Buchanan & Partners from 1964 to 1965.

Returning to London, Terry Farrell founded his practice in 1965 as a partnership with Nick Grimshaw, and has continued it in his own name since 1980. Over the past thirty years he has had considerable and diversified experience in architecture, urban design, planning and conservation, in all types of built projects and studies. Following his initial conceptual ideas, he has overall design control on each project through to completion, meeting regularly with the design directors and architects.

Terry Farrell has won many awards and lectured extensively in the United Kingdom and abroad, including the USA (UCLA, Columbia, Pennsylvania, Miami), Czechoslovakia, Germany, Hong Kong, Ireland, Japan and Norway. He has held teaching positions and/or has been a visiting tutor at the University of Cambridge, the Bartlett School of Architecture, the Architectural Association, the University of Strathclyde in Glasgow, the University of Sheffield and the University of Pennsylvania, USA. His work has been widely published and there have been eight major publications and books produced since 1984. A major exhibition was held at the RIBA's Heinz Gallery in 1987. He was awarded the Order of the British Empire (OBE) in 1979 for services to architecture.

In 1991 Terry Farrell opened an office in Hong Kong after winning the competition for the redevelopment of the Peak Tower and more recently the new headquarters for the British Consulate-General and the British Council, Kowloon Station and Kowloon Ventilation Building projects. In 1992 an office in Edinburgh was set up to manage the design and construction of the Edinburgh International Conference and Exhibition Centre. He is also working in conjunction with other architectural offices in France, Portugal, Malaysia, Sweden and Dubai. He has recently been awarded the American Institute of Architects 1994 Urban Design Award for the proposals for Paternoster Square in London.

Professional Affiliations
Member, Royal Institute of British Architects
Member, Royal Town Planning Institute
Fellow of the Chartered Society of Designers
Commissioner for English Heritage
Member, London Advisory Committee of English Heritage
Past Member, Historic Advisory Committee of English Heritage
Past President of the Urban Design Group
Past Member, RIBA Clients' Advisory Board
Past Member, RIBA Visiting Board
Past Member, RIBA Awards Panel
Architectural Assessor for Financial Times
    Architectural Awards, 1983
External Examiner, Royal College of Art
Member of the Royal Parks Review Group, 1991–1993
Consultant on *Architectural Design* Magazine

DOUGLAS STREETER
AA Dip., RIBA
Senior Design Director

Doug Streeter joined Terry Farrell & Company in 1979 and since then has worked directly with Terry Farrell on design development on numerous projects. These projects include Alban Gate, Brindleyplace, Charing Cross, Chiswick Park, Moor House, South Bank Arts Centre and Vauxhall Cross. More recently Doug has been designing and working in our Hong Kong office on the British Consulate General, The Peak, Kowloon Station and Kowloon Ventilation Building. Doug Streeter is Terry Farrell & Company's leading design director.

STEVEN SMITH
BA(Hons), Dip.Arch.
Design Director

Steve Smith joined Terry Farrell & Company in 1982 and since then has been involved in the early design stages of office, residential and master plan schemes, achieving planning consent on a number of complex projects on sensitive sites. These include the conversion and restoration of listed banking premises in Pall Mall, the Edinburgh International Conference and Exhibition Centre, Master plan for the South Bank Arts Centre, Kowloon Station in Hong Kong and also leading the Company Development Group in new work. More recently Steve has been working in Kuala Lumpur and the Middle East generating new work.

GARY YOUNG
BA(Hons), Dip.Arch., RIBA
Design Director

Gary Young joined Terry Farrell & Company in 1981 and since then has played a major part in the design of a number of key buildings. He has been in charge of design initiation, implementation and completion on two major projects involving complex listed building and building regulation consents— Comyn Ching Triangle and Tobacco Dock. Gary has also been responsible for the urban design of a number of master plans. These include Brindleyplace, Birmingham, Chester in Concert, Chiswick Park, the Edinburgh International Conference and Exhibition Centre, Hammersmith Island, King's Cross, Quarry Hill, Leeds and Thameslink 2000. More recently Gary has been working on our projects in Lisbon, Portugal.

DAVID BEYNON
BSc(Hons), Dip.Arch., RIBA
Project Director

David Beynon joined Terry Farrell & Company in 1986 and since then he has been involved through all stages of design and construction of the major and prestigious office development at Charing Cross. Responsibilities included organisation of submissions to statutory authorities, detailed design, overall management and contract administration. He is at present working on the Kowloon Station and Masterplan in Hong Kong, where he is responsible for fire strategy, specifications and building regulation issues of this large concourse and platform development.

NICHOLAS BIRCHALL
BA(Hons), Dip.Arch.(Cantab.)
Project Director

Nick Birchall joined Terry Farrell & Company in 1986 and since then his responsibilities have included overall management, detailed design and contract administration for a number of major projects. These include Alban Gate, an air-rights office development in London Wall from the planning submission stage to completion of the scheme; Vauxhall Cross Phase II fitout of 400,000-square-foot new government headquarters building; and Great Burgh, Surrey—100,000-square-foot new headquarters building for an international pharmaceutical company. More recently Nick coordinated the competition entry for Vasteras railway station in Sweden, Fort Canning Radio Tower in Singapore and is involved in business development for the company.

TOBY BRIDGE
BSc., Dip.Arch.(UCL), M.Arch., MCP(Berkeley), RIBA
Project Director

Toby Bridge joined Terry Farrell & Company in 1985 and since then has been project director on several large urban projects. These include in London—Embankment Place, an air-rights office development over Charing Cross Station and Vauxhall Cross, a government headquarters building fronting the River Thames. More recently Toby has been leading our Hong Kong office working on the Kowloon Station and master plan and generating new work in mainland China. Responsibilities include management and organisation of the detailed design and construction drawings of these complex and technically demanding projects, within very tight budgets and time scales.

SUSAN DAWSON
Dip.Arch., RIBA
Project Director

Susan Dawson joined Terry Farrell & Company in 1988 and since then has had responsibility for a number of major projects. These include the design and construction of the air-rights building over Charing Cross Station, the design and planning submission for the redevelopment of Moor House at London Wall obtained in 1991 and the overall coordination and implementation of the master plan for the redevelopment of Paternoster Square adjacent to St Paul's Cathedral. Since 1991 Susan has been responsible for business development of the company.

DEREK NOLAN
B.Arch., RIBA
Project Director

Derek Nolan joined Terry Farrell & Company in 1985 and has been involved in the major design and construction stages of several important projects. These include planning stage proposals for the Commonwealth Trust headquarters building, design proposals for Lloyds Bank, Pall Mall, reconstruction of a Grade II listed building and acting as project architect for Midland Bank, Fenchurch Street. Previously project director on Alban Gate, responsible for the development of the external cladding proposals for this major building, more recently Derek has been leading our Edinburgh office working on the Edinburgh International Conference and Exhibition Centre and generating new work in Scotland.

MICHAEL STOWELL
B.Arch., Reg.Arch.
Project Director

Mike Stowell joined Terry Farrell & Company in 1988 and since then has been involved in a number of major projects within the office. These include Alban Gate, where Mike was responsible for a large number of packages including the curtain walling and the supervision of associates and other architects; and Westminster Hospital, Horseferry Road, compiling the planning application. Mike coordinated the initial design development of The Peak Tower and the Headquarters for the British Consulate-General and the British Council, Hong Kong projects in London and more recently he has taken up the position of project director in our Hong Kong office, maintaining continuity and involvement with these projects.

BRIAN CHANTLER
FCA
Company Secretary

Brian Chantler joined Terry Farrell & Company in 1987 and has responsibility for the financial management and company administration. Professional indemnity insurance, appointment contracts, collateral warranties and other legal matters relating to projects or the company's business are also his responsibility. Recently he has been involved in establishing our offices in Edinburgh and Hong Kong and our associations with our practices in Malaysia and Portugal.

JOHN CAMPBELL
BSc(Hons), Arch.Dip.AA, RIBA
Technical Director

John Campbell joined Terry Farrell & Company in 1987 and since then has set up the technical department. He undertakes research, technical appraisals, preparation and coordination of specifications, establishment and witnessing of all tests for building components and products for our London, Edinburgh and Hong Kong offices. In particular, John specialises in cladding and curtain walling, quality control procedures and sub-contractor assessment.

Design Credits

Office Credits

London 1994
Stewart Abel
Karen Abrams
Stewart Armstrong
Teresa Ashton
Chris Barber
Nick Birchall
Andy Bow
John Campbell
Brian Chantler
Donna Clarke
Pamela Cronin
Andrew Culpeck
Susan Dawson
John Donnelly
Edmund Ellert
Graham Fairley
Terry Farrell
Jo Farrell
Sue Farrell
Grace Ford
Josephine Guckian
Lee Hallman
Jo Harrop
Nigel Horrell
Tom Horsford
Maggie Jones
Gillian Kearney
Spencer Kearnery
John Letherland
Martin Lilley
Euan MacKeller
Chris Moller
Giles Moore
Donal Murphy
Ike Ogbue
Eileen O'Reilly
Louise Parker
Arezoo Sadain
Helen Sexton
Roger Simmons
Martin Summersgill
Julian Tollast
Eugene Uys
Tim Warner
Vincent Westbrook
Chris Wood
Gary Young
Nigel Young

Edinburgh 1994
Dominique Andrews
Dorothy Batchelor
Neil De Prez
Derek Nolan
Dermot Patterson
Alexandra Stevens
Duncan Whatmore
Jes Worre

Hong Kong 1994
John Andrews
Mhairi Billinness
John Barber
Paul Bell
David Beynon
Toby Bridge
Steve Brown
Silvano Cranchi
Lau Chung Fai
Jaya Daswani
Gavin Erasmus
Tom Kimbell
Stefan Krummeck
Raymond Lee
Ellen Li
Stewart McLeod
John Riel
Malcolm Sage
Martin Sagar
Mark Shirburne-
    Davies
Mike Stowell
Doug Streeter
Letrice Tam
Tim Thompson
Mimi Tse
John Wakes
Iris Yuen

Kuala Lumpur 1994
Steve Smith

Lisbon 1994
Tony Davey

Over the years there have been many architects and staff who, although no longer with the practice, have contributed valuable work, including:
Sumati Ahuja
Titi Ajayi
Cormac Allen
Ken Allinson
Ashwin Amin
Keith Anderson
Chris Anglin
Simon Appleby
Page Ayres
Laurence Bain
Tony Balmbra
Sumaya Bardawil
Chuck Barguirdjian
Alistair Barr
Nick Barratt-Boyes
Steve Barton
Christian Bechtle
Rosalyn Bell
Neil Bennett
Marc Berg
Maggie Bernard
Emma Birkett
Brian Borschoff

Greg Boyden
Andy Brown
Ray Bryant
Mike Burgess
Sally Burkhart
Matthew Burling
Paul Burnham
James Burrell
Helen Carroll
Francesca Carta
Helen Chandler
Kim Chatterley
John Chatwin
Philip Chester
David Chetwin
David Clarke
Guy Cleverley
Arturo Cogollo
Richard Cohen
Kevin Cook
Frank Cooney
Mike Cooper
Jim Corcoran
Alan Corrigan
Andrew Cowan
Andrew Cowser
Tom Creed
Aaron Crosby
Christian Cuhls
Andrew Culham
Julia Dawson
Manus Deery
Aubrey Dick
Michael Donovan
Craig Downie
Michael Doyle
Barbara Draper
Lana Durovic
Lisa Dwyer
Marianne Dykes
James Edwards
Kris Ellam
Helen Espey
Tim Evans
Gerard Evenden
Chris Farrell
Tye Farrow
D'Arcy Fenton
Jacques Ferrier
Kevin Finn
Nigel Fitton
John Fitzgerald
Mark Floate
Joe Foges
Carol Foster
Lionel Friedland
Les Fuller
Mike Gallagher
Anne Galloway
Sharon Galvin
Christian Garnett
David Gausden
Rosie Gawthorp
Paul Gibson
Joanne Gillis

David Gillooley
Michael Glass
John Grant
Emma Gribble
Lee Guilfoyle
Trevor Hall
Caroline Hambury
Chris Hannan
Kai Hansen
Jonathon Harford
Helen Harker
Sarah Haskell
Geraldine Herrity
Jan Heynike
Michael Hickey
Frank Hickson
Gaby Higgs
Lizzie Hill
Stephen Hill
Andrew Hobson
Sue Hollick
Jeremy Hoskyn
Vicky Hoyle
Simon Hudspith
Peter Hulbert
David Hunt
Steve Ibbotson
Maria Iwanicki
Barry James
Robert James
Mike Jarman
David Jenkins
Peter Jenkins
David Jennings
Tom Jestico
Mike Johnson
Frank Kavanagh
Mary Kelly
Jane Kille
Lisa Kingston
Sebastian Klatt
Elke Knoesz
Marcus Kuhn
Colin Laine
Stella Lancashire
John Langley
Paul Langolis
Martin Lazenby
Barbara Le Blanc
David Leece
Mark Lecchini
Colin Leisk
Kevin Lewendon
Shane Lincoln
Mark Lloyd-Davis
Peter Locke
Simon Loring
Julia Lowery
Jim Luke
Caroline Lwin
Ian Macduff
Barry Macken
Robert Malcolm
Janet Male
Nick Marcucci

James Marshall
Steve Marshall
Sue Martin
Antonio Martinez
Campbell McAlister
Stephen McCrane
Stephen McDougall
Jonathan McDowell
Peter McGirr
Ian McKim
Anne-Marie
    McMahon
Brian Meeke
Paul Mollard
Alan Morris
Peter Morris
Justin Mueller
Tom Mulligan
Paul Murphy
Andrew Ng
Catherine Norman
Jo Odgers
Ian Orr
Maurice Orr
Zvonko Orsanic
Richard Paine
Annie Palmer
Dominic Papa
Christos Papaloizou
David Parken
Jonathan Parkinson
Gaye Patel
Satish Patel
Gareth Paterson
Terry Pawson
Jeremy Peacock
Beverley Pearce
John Petrarca
Sharon Phillips
Tom Phillips
James Pickard
Elizabeth Pienaar
Chen Pi Hsueh
Janelle Plummer
Laurie Pocza
Tom Politowicz
Neil Porter
Louise Potter
Claus Preisen
David Quigley
Claudine Railton
Amir Ramezani
Manoja Ranawake
Nicholas Rank
Paul Rayer
Thierry Reinhardt
Oliver Richards
Thomas Ringhof
Alex Ritchie
Drummond Robson
Louise Rokosh
Paul Rolph
Anne Rose
Shaun Russell
Edward Rutherfoord

Finonuala Ryan
Keith Sagar
Graham Saunders
Lee Schmidtchen
Rollin Schlicht
Ed Scott
Ian Scott
Walter Seward
Graham Sharpe
Tony Sharplanin
Ray Shiels
Ron Sidell
Chris Simmans
Rick Skenzell
Doug Smith
Julia Smith
Philip Smithies
Alan Smith-Oliver
Richard Solomon
Neil Southard
David Spillane
Matthew Stannard
Andrew Stavart
Karl Stedman
Neil Stevenson
Ian Stewart
Barry Stobbs
Simon Sturgis
Carolyn Sullivan-Paul
Kevin Sullivan
Nick Swannell
Greg Talmont
Richard Tan
Emma Tapping
Colin Taylor
Kate Taylor
Mike Taylor
Roy Tellings
Ashok Tendle
Mike Thompson
Peter Tigg
Nick Toft
Tim Tolcher
Ivan Turcinov
Fenella Upson
Dewar Van
    Antwerpen
Elizabeth Vandertuin
Jane Visser
Jon Wallsgrove
Kim Ward
Geoff Warn
Mike Warren
Sarah Wick
Clive Wilkinson
Ros Wilkinson
Ed Williams
Keith Williams
Clare Wincote
Simon Wing
Robert Wood
Katie Woodruff
Stefan Zalewski
Giuliano Zampi

Associates & Collaborators

Collaborators

Robert Adam
Tom Beeby
David Binns
Andrew Birds
Derek Brentnall
Lauren Butt
Chris Colbourne
Miguel Correia
DEGW
Vilma Gianini
Paul Gibson
Bosco Ho
Simon Hudspith
Steve Ibbotson
Charles Jencks
Tom Jestico
Rolfe Judd
Maggie Keswick
Tryfon Kalyvides
Ralph Lebens
Kamil Merican
Laurie Olin
Richard Portchmouth
David Quigley
Peter Rice
Ian Ritchie
RMJM
Mike Russim
John Simpson
Dr Peter Smith
Simon Sturgis

Chronological List of Buildings & Projects

*Indicates work featured in this book
(see Selected and Current Works).

With Farrell/Grimshaw Partnership

*International Students Hostel
1965–1968
Sussex Gardens, Paddington, London W2

*125 Park Road
1968–1970
Marylebone, London NW8
Mercury Housing Society
Forty co-owner flats

Children's Home
1970
St Christopher's Fellowship

Runnymede Warehouse
1972–1973
Runnymede, Berkshire, England

Rehabilitation Study of 1,000 Older Council-owned Dwellings
1975
City of Westminster, London

*The Colonnades, Porchester Square
1974–1976
Bishops Bridge Road, London W2

Herman Miller Factory
1975–1976
Bath, Avon, England

BMW Distribution Centre
1978–1979
Administration Headquarters for BMW
Bracknell, Berkshire, England

*Maunsel Housing Society
1972–1980
Greater London
Maunsel Housing Society
A range of small-scale low-cost schemes in backland and infill sites.

With Terry Farrell & Company

*Clifton Nurseries, Bayswater
1979–1980
Bishops Bridge Road, London W2

*Oakwood Housing
1978–1981
Warrington New Town, Warrington, England

Digital Factory Conversion
1979–1981
Reading, Berkshire, England

*Clifton Nurseries, Covent Garden
1980–1981
Covent Garden, London WC2

*Urban Infill Factories, Wood Green
1979–1981
Wood Green, Haringey, London N22

*Crafts Council Gallery
1980–1981
Waterloo Place, London WC2

*Alexandra Pavilion
1980–1981
Alexandra Park, Haringey, London N22

*Private House, Lansdowne Walk
1979–1982
Holland Park, London W11
Designed together with Charles Jencks and Maggie Keswick

*Garden Festival Exhibition Building
1982
Liverpool, England
Competition entry

*Water Treatment Centre
1979–1982
Reading, Berkshire, England
Thames Water Authority

Private House
1981–1982
St John's Wood, London
Jacob Rothschild and family

*TVam Breakfast Television Studios
1981–1982
Camden, London NW1

Effra Redevelopment National Competition
1982
Vauxhall, London SE1
Competition entry

Radio Headquarters for the British Broadcasting Corporation
1982–1983
Langham Place, Portland Place, London W1
Competition entry

*Limehouse Television Studios
1982–1983
West India Docks, London E14

Royal Opera House Study
1980–1984
Covent Garden, London WC2

Graphex Industrial Design
1982–1984
South Acton, London W3

Hammersmith Island Study
1984
Hammersmith Broadway, London W6
Greater London Council and local residents
Study

The Triangles, Mansion House Square Study
1984
Mansion House Square, London, EC4
SAVE and English Heritage
Study

*Comyn Ching Triangle
1978–1985
Seven Dials, Covent Garden, London WC2

*Allied Irish Bank, Queen Street
1982–1985
Queen Street, London, EC4

*Henley Royal Regatta Headquarters
1983–1985
Henley-on-Thames, Berkshire, England

*Midland Bank, Fenchurch Street
1983–1986
Fenchurch Street, London EC3

Rules Restaurant
1985–1986
Covent Garden, London WC2

East Putney Station
1983–1987
East Putney, London SW18

Penthouses for The Savoy Hotel
1986–1987
The Strand, London WC2
Project

*King's Cross Master Plan
1987
Kings Cross, London NW1
Study

Port Greenwich Master Plan
1988
East Greenwich, London SE10
Study

Brentford Dock Master Plan
1988
London Borough of Hounslow
Study

Carlton Gardens
1988
London SW1
Competition entry

Hospital Redevelopment Master Plan
1988
Bloomsbury Health Authority Hospitals
City of Westminster and London
Borough of Camden
Study

Office Building, 3–5 Norwich Street
1986–1988
London EC4

Wimbledon Town Centre Master Plan
1987–1988
Wimbledon, London SWI9
Study

Architects Offices, 17 Hatton Street
1985–1988
London NW8
Terry Farrell & Company

Frankfurt Flughafen, Germany
1989
Airport Master Plan and New
Administration Offices
Competition entry

Garosud Master Plan
1990
Montpellier, France
Study

Lockmeadow Master Plan
1990
Lockmeadow, Maidstone
Study

*Tobacco Dock
1985–1990
Shopping village and historic
building restoration
Pennington Street, Wapping, London E1

*South Bank Arts Centre
1985–1990
Public exhibition 1989
South Bank, London SE1

*Embankment Place
1987–1990
1 Embankment Place, Villiers Street,
London WC2

Lloyds Bank
1990
Lombard Street, London EC3
Project

*Temple Island
1988–1991
Restoration of historic building by Wyatt
Henley-on-Thames

Tower Hill Wine Vaults
1989–1991
Restoration and tourist/shopping
complex
Tower Hill, London EC3

**Director, Thames Study for the Royal Fine
Arts Commission**
1991
Public Exhibition

*Commonwealth Trust Offices and Club
1991
Northumberland Avenue, London WC1
Project

*Lloyds Bank Headquarters, Pall Mall
1991
Waterloo Place, London WC2
Project

Spitalfields Market Master Plan Study
1991
Spitalfields, London E1
SAVE

*Moor House
1991
London Wall, London EC2

*Alban Gate
1987–1992
125 London Wall, London EC2

*Fort Canning Radio Tower, Singapore
1992
Competition entry

***Government Headquarters Building
(MI6), Vauxhall Cross**
1988–1993
Albert Embankment, London SE1

*Thameslink 2000, Master Plan
Infrastructure design and Blackfriars
Bridge Station
1991–1993
Thameslink 2000/British Rail
Study

**New Headquarters Complex for Smith
Kline Beecham**
1993
Great Burgh, Epsom, Surrey, England
Project

*Braehead Retail Complex Master Plan
1993
Braehead, Glasgow
Marks & Spencer PLC and
J. Sainsbury PLC
Competition entry

Ongoing Schemes and Projects

*Westminster Hospital Redevelopment, Horseferry Road
1991–1994
St John's Gardens, Horseferry Road, London SW1
Mixed-use planning study

South Kensington Underground Station and Mixed-use Development
1991–1994
Public exhibition 1993
South Kensington, London SW7

*New National Gallery of Scottish Art and History
1993–1994
Kelvingrove Park, Glasgow
Study

*Sainsbury's Supermarket
1992–1994
Fourth & Fifth Ave, Harlow, Essex

*Edinburgh International Conference and Exhibition Centre/Master Plan
1989–1995
Morrison Street, Edinburgh, Scotland
Winning competition entry

56–72 Grey Street, Newcastle
1991–1995
Urban regeneration

*The Peak Tower, Hong Kong
1991–1995
Winning competition entry

*Kowloon Ventilation Building, Hong Kong
1993–1995
Kowloon, Hong Kong
Mass Transit Railway Corporation

Master Plan Study and New Ferry Terminal
1993–1995
Barreiro, Lisbon, Portugal
Lisbon Railways

Vasteras Railway Station, Sweden
1993–1995
Winning competition entry
New railway station and associated master plan

*Headquarters for the British-Consulate General and the British Council, Hong Kong
1992–1996
Supreme Court Road, Hong Kong
Winning competition entry

*Library and Cultural Centre, Dubai
1993–1995
Winning competition entry

*Kowloon Station, Hong Kong
1992–1997
Kowloon, Hong Kong
Mass Transit Railway Corporation
Winning competition entry

New Railway Station and associated development for British Rail
Cross Rail: Farringdon
1991- 1998

Quarry Hill Master Plan
1989–
Quarry Hill, Leeds
Landscaping completed 1994

*Paternoster Square Master Plan
1989–
Paternoster Square, London EC4
Infrastructure design and individual office buildings

*Chiswick Park Master Plan
1989
Chiswick, London W4
Infrastructure design and individual office buildings
Landscaping completed 1992

*Brindleyplace Master Plan
1990–

East Quayside Master Plan, Newcastle
1991–

Castlegate Development, York
1991–

Chester in Concert
1993–
Chester, Cheshire
Concert hall and regional arts centre

Awards & Exhibitions

Awards

Terry Farrell & Company has been the recipient of many awards and commendations, some of which are listed below.

AIA Award for Urban Design
American Institute of Architects, USA
1994

European Structural Steel Award
1993

Construction Industry Award
Runner Up: 1991

RIBA Awards
1991, 1988, 1980, 1978
RIBA National Award: 1991
RIBA Commendations: 1983, 1981, 1975

Award for Planning Achievement
RTPI
Commendation: 1991

Civic Trust Awards
1991, 1988, 1987, 1981, 1978
Commendation: 1985

Structural Steel Design Awards
1991, 1977, 1969

Ambrose Congreve Award, USA
1984

International Interiors Award, USA
1984

Architectural Design Project Awards
1983, 1982

Business and Industry Awards
Highly commended: 1981, 1977

Housing Awards
Department of the Environment
1981, 1977

TCPA/Guardian New Community Award
1980

Financial Times Architecture Award
1977
Commendations: 1987, 1980

RICS/The Times Conservation Award
Commendation: 1976

Exhibitions

Building the South Bank: 1753–1993
South Bank Arts Centre Study
The Architecture Foundation,
London SW1
February–March 1994
The Royal Festival Hall, South Bank
May 1994

L'Architecture des batiments des medias
Pavillon de l'Arsenal, Paris
May–August 1994

Terry Farrell: New Work
Terry Farrell office, London NW8
April–May 1994

Terry Farrell: Urban Design
Edinburgh, Leeds, Glasgow, Newcastle,
London
1993–1994

City Changes: Architecture in the City of London 1985–1995
Moor House
The Architecture Foundation in
association with the Corporation
of London
The Royal Exchange Building,
London EC2
San Paolo Biennal, Brazil
August–September 1993
50th Anniversary Celebrations of the
British Council in Barcelona, Spain
September–December 1993
Prague, Czechoslovakia
Spring 1994

A Vision of Europe
Henley Royal Regatta Headquarters and
Paternoster Square
University of Bologna, Italy
September 1992

Paternoster Square Public Exhibition
Paternoster Square, London EC
May–June 1991

Post-Modern Exhibition
Organised by Architectural Design
Landmark House, London NW1
June 1991

The Royal Fine Art Commission: Thames Study
The Thames Study initiative,
commissioned and exhibited by the Royal
Fine Art Commission, was led and
co-ordinated by Terry Farrell
The Royal Fine Art Commission, London
May 1991

Public Spaces—London goes West
Chiswick Park Master Plan and
Hammersmith Island Study
The Emerald Centre, London W16
October 1991

History, Design and Construction: Tobacco Dock
Tobacco Dock, London
March–December 1989

Completing the Vision: Proposals for the South Bank
Royal Festival Hall, London SE
March 1989

Edinburgh International Conference Centre: Early Studies
Davis Langdon & Everest Exhibition of
Recent Architectural Proposals
The Design Museum, London
May 1989

British Week
The Redevelopment of Charing Cross
Organised by SKALA and the Danish
Association of Architects
Aalborg, Denmark
September–October 1989

Terry Farrell: In the Context of London
Royal Institute of British Architects
Heinz Gallery, London W1
May–June 1987

British Architecture Today Touring Exhibition
Japan
September–October 1987

British Architecture 1982
Organised by Architectural Design
Royal Institute of British Architects,
London
August 1982

Venice Biennial
1981

Bibliography

Selected General Articles by Terry Farrell

"Design Matters." Monthly column in *RIBA Journal* (UK, April–December 1983).

"A Designer's Approach to Rehabilitation—Three Inner London Cases." In Thomas A. Markus (ed.). *Building Conversion and Rehabilitation: Design for Change in Building Use.* Newnes-Butterworth, 1979.

"Enter the Edge"—The Royal Parks." *Landscape Design* (UK, December 1992/January 1993): pp. 17–18.

"Heroes & Villains—Frank Lloyd Wright by Terry Farrell." *Independent* magazine (UK, June 8, 1991): p. 70.

"The Louis Kahn Studio at the University of Pennsylvania." *Arena* (March 1967).

"Mario Botta: The Complete Works, Volume 1." (Book review) *World Architecture* (UK, no. 26, 1993): pp. 104–105.

"Michael Graves: Building and Projects 1966–1981." (Book review) *Building* (UK, September 2, 1981).

"My Kind of Town." *Architecture Today* (UK, no. 44, January 1994): p. 48.

"Pop Architecture—A Sophisticated Interpretation of Popular Culture?" Academy International Forum on POPular Architecture, at the Royal Academy of Arts, London, 16 November 1991. *Architectural Design* (UK, vol. 62, no. 7/8, July/August 1992): pp. 37–38.

"Post-Modern Urbanism." *Art & Design* (UK, February 1985): pp. 16–19. Abridged transcript of a lecture given to the Urban Design Group, 16 October 1984.

Selected Articles, Farrell/Grimshaw Partnership

"Buildings as a Resource—Architectural Association Lecture." *RIBA Journal* (UK, May 1976).

"Farrell/Grimshaw Recent Work." *Architectural Design* (UK, February 1973).

"The Men Most Likely To." *Building Design* (UK, 25 February 1972).

"Setting up Practice." *Architects' Journal* (UK, January 1971).

"Survival by Design: RIBA Lecture—Architects' Approach to Architecture." *RIBA Journal* (UK, October 1974).

"Whatever Happened to the Systems Approach?" *Architectural Design* (UK, May 1979).

Selected Articles about the Practice

"After-Modernist: Terry Farrell." *City Magazine* (Hong Kong, April/May 1992): pp. 108–115.

"The Air Rights Building: Symbol of a New London—The Redevelopment of Charing Cross." *Office Age* (Japan, no. 16, 1991): pp. 50–55.

"Architect on the Scene." *Kenchiku Bunka* (Japan, April 1994).

"The Architect's Seven-year Itch." *Estates Gazette* (UK, October 30, 1993): pp. 50–51.

"Around the City with Terry Farrell." *Blueprint* (UK, no. 27, May 1986): pp. 28–33.

"Attitudes of an Anglo-Saxon." *Architects' Journal* (UK, November 10, 1982).

"Batiment de Services pour la Thames Water Authority." *l'Architecture d'Aujourd'hui* (France, September 1983): pp. 84–89.

"Best Products—Lateral Thinking." *Architects' Journal* (UK, November 25, 1981).

"Capital Asset." Building Design (May 10, 1991): pp. 17–24.

"Changing Places—Edinburgh International Conference Centre." *Building Design* (UK, June 4, 1993).

"Classicismo Britannico." *Casa Oggi* (Italy, September 1992): pp. 36–49.

"Colour Confessions by Contemporary Architects." *Daidalos* (Germany, March 1994): p. 43.

"Cornering the City—Fenchurch Street & Seven Dials." *Architects' Journal,* (UK, June 15, 1988): pp. 35–49.

"Designing a House." *Architectural Design Profile* (no. 9/10, 1986).

"Due sulla piazza–Alban Gate." *Costruire* (Italy, no. 107, April 1992): pp. 164–167.

"Farrell Moves Towards Symbolism." by Charles Jencks. *British Architecture.* London: Academy Editions, 1982.

"Gateway to the City: Terry Farrell on London Wall." *Architecture Today* (UK, no. 29, June 1992).

"Jewel of the Thames—The Redevelopment of Charing Cross." *The World & I* (USA, February 1992): pp. 176–181.

London: A Guide to Recent Architecture. London: Artemis, 1993.

"London Architecture—Paternoster Square and The Redevelopment of Charing Cross." *Nikkei Architecture* (Japan, vol, 12, no. 9, 1991): pp. 123, 131–139.

"London Wall Spanned—Alban Gate." *Building* (UK, June 19, 1992): pp. 37–43.

"The Man Who Took High Tech Out To Play." *Sunday Times Magazine* (UK, January 16, 1983).

"New Town Goes West." *RIBA Journal* (UK, April 1993): pp. 18–21.

"Post-Modern Triumphs in London." *Architectural Design Profile* (no. 91, 1991).

"Pragmatic Classicism." *Domus* (Italy, July 1981).

"Racing Ahead—Henley Royal Regatta Headquarters." *Architectural Record* (USA, November 1986): pp. 118–123.

"Reflections on Farrell." *Architects' Journal* (UK, August 19, 1981).

"Special Report: Terry Farrell." *at magazine* (Japan, July 1992): pp. 33–39.

"Terry Farrell: Building in Wren's Shadow." *Blueprint* (UK, no. 79, July/August 1991): pp. 28–31.

"Tobacco Dock–New Leaf." *Architectural Record* (USA, February 1994): pp 112–117.

"Tobacco Trader." *Architects' Journal* (UK, December 13, 1989): pp. 32–53.

"The Total Terry Farrell." *Estates Gazette* (UK, May 10, 1986): pp. 567–568.

"Uber den Gleisen von Charing Cross." *Bauwelt* (Germany, no. 46, December 4, 1992): pp. 2596–2603.

"Un nuovo monumento: Vauxhall Cross." *Ufficiostile* (Italy, November 1993): pp. 50–59.

"Urban Reflections: Terry Farrell at Vauxhall Cross." *Architecture Today* (UK, no. 38, May 1993): pp. 24–30.

World Cities: London. London: Academy Group Ltd, 1993.

Major Publications and Books

Lightweight Classic: Terry Farrell's Covent Garden Nursery Building. London: World Architecture Building Profile No. 1, 1993.

Palace on the River: Terry Farrell's Design for the Redevelopment of Charing Cross. London: Wordsearch Publishing, 1991.

Terry Farrell. London/New York: Academy Editions/St Martin's Press, 1984.

Terry Farrell: In the Context of London. London: Production by Blueprint Magazine, 1987.

"Terry Farrell." *A+U* Special feature (Japan, December 1989): pp. 37–132.

Terry Farrell: Urban Design. London; Academy Group, 1993.

"*Blueprint Extra No. 9—Three Urban Projects*", London: Wordsearch Publishing, 1993.

Vauxhall Cross: The Story of the Design and Construction of a New London Landmark. London: Wordsearch Publishing, 1992.

Acknowledgments

Jo Farrell was responsible for the organisation of this book within Terry Farrell's office, and our many thanks to her for bringing order to a wide range of projects and visual material.

The text is by Clare Melhuish.

The projects cover such an extended period of the work of Terry Farrell's office, that it is impossible to include here all those who have been involved. In the early years, until 1979, Terry's partner was Nick Grimshaw who was a great inspiration and a valued, close friend. Of special note are: John Chatwin, who was Terry's partner for 12 years and, particularly during the early years played a very key role, and Ashok Tendle, who was Joint Managing Director for 5 years; his experience, wisdom and management skills were an inspiration to us all.

The office is organised on the basis that Terry Farrell is in charge of all design and overall direction of the work. The senior Design Director, who has been with Terry Farrell since the late 1970s and is involved in almost all office projects, is Douglas Streeter. On the master planning side are Design Directors Steve Smith and Gary Young. Philip Smithies has also been involved as Design Director in many key projects in recent years. Past Design Directors in particular include Clive Wilkinson and Simon Sturgis. Project Directors take overall charge of implementing each project and among these are the following who have been involved in the projects covered in this book and without them the planning, organisation and broad technical and architectural overview of the individual projects would not have been implemented; their work has been and continues to be invaluable: David Beynon, Nick Birchall, Toby Bridge, Susan Dawson, Derek Nolan, Mike Stowell.

Within the office Brian Chantler is the Company Secretary and John Campbell is overall Technical Director. Other key staff include Stuart Armstrong, Andy Bow, Steven Brown, Graham Fairley, Tryfon Kalyvides, John Letherland, Martin Sagar, Martin Summersgill, Tim Thompson, Julian Tollast, Eugene Uys, Duncan Whatmore, Chris Wood and Jes Worre.

Susan Farrell plays an important role in assisting Terry Farrell's architectural overview and is involved in her own role as an artist and painter, in the colouration work on projects, as well as leading on the selection of artists and craftspersons on the public domain of our master plans. All the names mentioned above are senior staff at Associate level and above. Of particular importance to us is Nigel Young who, apart from his creative architectural and urban design contribution, has taken many of the best photographs included in this book. There are many more who have made important contributions but space does not allow inclusion of all their names. On a personal level, Maggie Jones is Terry Farrell's secretary and personal assistant and has made a most invaluable contribution for over 25 years.

There are also senior people no longer with us who made important contributions, including Ken Allinson, Alastair Barr, Neil Bennett, Ray Bryant, David Clarke, Mike Cooper, Alan Corrigan, Andrew Cowan, Craig Downie, Nigel Fitton, John Fitzgerald, Joe Foges, Paul Gibson, John Grant, Caroline Hambury, Steve Ibbotson, Robert James, Tom Jestico, Colin Laine, John Langley, Kevin Lewendon, Ian Macduff, Steve Marshall, John Petrarca, David Quigley, Nicholas Rank, Oliver Richards, Edward Rutherfoord, Drummond Robson, Graham Saunders, Rollin Schlicht, Ron Sidell, Barry Stobbs, Kate Taylor, Jon Wallsgrove and Simon Wing.

Mention should also be made of Harvey van Sickle, who does all the historical research, and the photographers over the years who have given much pleasure to us in the office with their visual record of our work.

Finally, many thanks to the clients, consultants, builders and suppliers, local government officers and numerous other parties, this broad cast of other disciplines with whom we combine and work to make each project a reality.

Index

Bold page numbers refer
to projects included in
Selected and Current Works.